SOCIALISM AND SURVIVAL

also by Rudolf Bahro:

The Alternative in Eastern Europe (Verso/NLB)

This book is the first title from Heretic Books,
a publisher of the independent left. For details
of our future programme, write to P O Box 247,
London N15 6RW.

Rudolf Bahro

Socialism and Survival

(articles, essays and talks 1979-1982)

introduced by
E.P. Thompson

heretic books hb

This volume contains a selection of the texts first collected in book form in *Elemente einer neuen Politik*, together with the previously unpublished 'Conditions for a Socialist Perspective in the Late Twentieth Century', 'Reply to Three Questions from the West German Radio' and 'Who Can Stop the Apocalypse?'

This edition first published October 1982 by Heretic Books, P O Box 247, London N15 6RW, England.

British Library/Library of Congress Cataloguing in Publication Data

Bahro, Rudolf
    Socialism and survival: articles, essays and
    talks 1979-1982.
    1. Socialism
    I. Title   II. Elemente einer neuen
    Politik. *English*
    335   HX44
    ISBN 0 946097 02 X
    ISBN 0 946097 00 3 Pbk

20026179

Translation and editing: David Fernbach
Cover: Louis Mackay
Design and make-up: Aubrey Walter

335

Photoset by Shanta Thawani, 25 Natal Road, London N11 2HU
Printed and bound by Book Plan (Billing & Sons Ltd.), Worcester

Introduction by E.P. Thompson

For some odd reason, Rudolf Bahro thought it might be helpful if this collection of his recent writings was presented to the English-speaking public by a native. I am honoured that the lot should have fallen to me, but any extended introduction is unnecessary. It would only get in the way. Bahro's reputation is secure. It rests upon *The Alternative in Eastern Europe,* one of the few necessary, original, and truly significant contributions to the political thought of Europe in the post-War years.

That book was researched and written in East Germany, in the years 1972 to 1977, in Bahro's spare time, while he was working as an industrial administrator or political manager. Educated in the German Marxist (and Communist) traditions, he brought the method of Marx and the principles of Rosa Luxemburg to bear upon the analysis of 'actually existing socialism' . I will not describe the book further, since it is, and will long remain, essential reading.

The Alternative was published by a West German trade-union publishing house. Bahro was duly arrested, accused of publishing 'state secrets' (!), and sentenced to eight years' imprisonment. He was correctly treated in prison, got through a great deal of reading (including the Bible, from end to end), began to teach himself French and English, and was eventually released, more than two years later, to West Germany.

The present volume takes up the story at that point. The 'story' is the subsequent development of Rudolf Bahro's political thought. This requires no interpreter, and I will content myself with two comments.

First, Bahro's originality asserts itself in the manner in which he breaks free from every stereotype and disappoints the expectations of most of the reception committees eagerly awaiting him in the 'free West' . To simplify, 'dissidents' from the 'East' are normally received with three kinds of expectation. First, there are the very well-funded and experienced Cold War operators, supported by Western intelligence: these stand ready to receive and sort the dissenters, grade them by weight, and pass them along the line to visiting fellowships in Western universities or the like. Second, there are the eager (but usually impoverished and materially unhelpful) reception groups of various zealous political movements — some of them Marxist and Trotskyist — whose hands are held out anxiously to claim the newcomer as one of their own. Third, there is a gentler, less calculating, reception network among refugee compatriots and others who simply expect the newcomer to lie low for a while, to find a new place in life, and who advise an interval for rehabilitation and reflection before attempting any intervention.

Bahro disappointed all three sets of expectation. Like someone leaping from a moving train, he hit the ground running, but running in his own direction. He had no interest in taking part in Cold War games. This is partly because he refuses *both* 'sides' — the very notion of 'sides' is specious. He does not nourish bitterness against the GDR, and he often insists that there are large (if hidden) constituencies to address on 'the other side' . It is partly also because the malaise which he had identified in Eastern Europe he found also in the West.

Bahro did not identify himself with any of the eagerly awaiting Marxist groups. But he did not repudiate or denounce them either. He acknowledged the socialist tradition, and the tradition of Marx, but he went on to challenge some of its most sacred categories (including that of 'class' , and of humankind's relation to nature), or the relevance of those categories in the present. He identified himself with the new ecological movement, the 'Greens' , and he sought to bring the different socialist fractions together into a more generous 'Socialist Conference' . He came from the GDR with a prophetic sense of urgency, and by deliberate choice he allowed himself no time for 'rehabilitation' or reflection. He chose to think in public and on his feet. This book is the product of these public exchanges.

My second comment is this. Bahro's vision, which does not refuse the utopian mode (it was sad also to note that in 'actually existing socialism' a writer could be imprisoned for the passion of his socialist utopianism) is fresh and original. And yet, in a surprising way, it is traditional also. When I read the third and final section of *The Alternative,* I was astonished to find, on page after page, a reincarnation in modern dress of some of the essential preoccupations of William Morris in his socialist writings of the 1880s. Yet Morris's socialist essays were unknown to Bahro. It is encouraging to know that this vision, fresh and with new additions, wells up once again.

Since Rudolf Bahro completed most of the essays which make up this book he has been increasingly committed (and distracted from his primary themes) by the urgent work for European nuclear disarmament. He has played an outstanding part in advising the peace movement in West Germany and in assisting us all in our relations with Eastern Europe. It is good to have him as a friend and colleague.

Preface to the German Edition

When I first arrived in the West, some people — even people who were familiar with my writing and had not just heard of me through the media — were worried or actually disappointed that I did not prefer at first to maintain a cautious silence, while analysing things carefully and in particular keeping aloof from political parties. I should as it were have withdrawn from the fray and tried — guided by books, personal discussion and the experience of daily life — to get to know the situation here as well as I understood conditions in East Germany before pronouncing on them. It was only to be expected, of course, that my immediate political involvement would not merely be physically and mentally exhausting, but would also bring with it a loss of innocence as far as the internal politics of West Germany are concerned.

After everything that led up to my arrival, however, it would not only have been difficult, but in my view inappropriate, had I not shown myself from the start as the political person that I am and remain. For the sake of the cause I had committed myself to, I needed first of all to correct the image that the mass media had presented of me. I was never an 'East German dissident' in the sense that even the supposedly serious press liked to portray me. I hadn't arrived in the West just to insult the GDR from a safe distance, or to confirm the self-righteous prejudices of people who like to sit around and casually compare the two social systems.

The common prejudice cultivated by reactionaries here shares to a remarkable degree the view of the political bureaucracy in the GDR that criticism of its regime is necessarily directed at the liquidation of the East German state, if not of the entire society. What was understood in the case of the Czech reformers of 1968, or at least realistically accepted — that they did not seek to destroy the foundations on which they stood, but simply to transform the institutional superstructure and achieve a socialism with a human face — is only conceded to the opposition in the GDR by an enlightened minority, chiefly on the left. And anyone whose sympathy for this opposition means above all else the desire for 'reunification' — even if they imagine the result as social-democratic or radical-democratic — only gives the ruling apparatus there a better right to call books such as mine 'counter-revolutionary'.

It is in the interest of all political forces on both sides of the frontier, if they perceive this correctly, to finally accept that conditions on the other side will not change as the result of models introduced from outside, since only too often these betray the limitations of their own horizon. In this regard, thinking in the East is significantly more advanced, even at top levels. In West Germany, however, far too many people like to forget, firstly, that the border between the Eastern and Western blocs which has run through Germany since the Soviet-American 'meeting on the Elbe' is the result of a national history that went astray; secondly, that it can no longer be overcome within the German context, i.e. without a dismantling of the confrontation between East and West; and thirdly, that this will also require other far-reaching changes on both sides. The East German population would only exchange the frying-pan for the fire if a socio-political change were simply to give them the same conditions we have here — not to speak of the dangers involved in any shift in the balance of forces. And so right from the start I have taken my distance from those who welcomed my fundamental critique of the other social order simply as a weapon in their psychological warfare.

Besides, public opinion in a country faced with the arrival of someone they've been told a bit about has a right to know precisely what his position is. And it's not as if I have moved to a foreign country. Much as the GDR was my homeland, and I have no intention of discarding what my life there gave me, I now intend to make myself at home as a citizen, in the widest sense, of this Federal Republic; i.e. to be just as responsible as I was over there. I intend to continue my path in the same direction that I pursued in the GDR with my critique of 'actually existing socialism' and the proposal of an alternative. At the same time, I am well aware that this is possible only with a certain re-examination of my former standpoints (the very word indicates how easy it is to get stuck in one's positions, instead of being on the move) and attitudes (which are even more deeply rooted in personal biography than are standpoints). The texts collected here were what I had immediately available, and should be read as nothing more than an outline. They document an attitude, an orientation towards problems, rather than a definitive conclusion. I arrived in West Germany with only a sketchy position, and this still needs substantial elaboration.

The core of my position, in other words, is not based on any immediate experience of conditions in the West. In the first place, though, I can say that in the GDR people know far more about West Germany than the other way round, and it has always been possible for someone to find out many important things about a country without living in it (just as a historian can know such things at a distance in time). I could add in case people are interested that in 1946, at the age of ten, I spent several months in a village near Biedenkopf an der Lahn [in West Germany]. Naturally, I have always taken a very conscious interest in what has been happening 'over here'. In this connection I was not so much interested in the other German state for its own sake, but rather as a part of the First World, the late-capitalist metropolitan alliance, in which of course West Germany plays a particular role.

If I felt more or less at home right away in this very different world, that was possible because I perceived the situation in Eastern Europe, too, as part of a wider whole. My assumption is that the history of the Soviet Union since 1917, and the history of Eastern Europe since the Second World War, can only be understood if they are treated as a response to the challenge posed by capitalist industrialism. Although Marx's work, which governed my intellectual formation, does not offer sufficient knowledge about capitalism today, it still gives us a basic knowledge of capitalism; and the new developments have naturally been noticed in East Germany and taken into account.

The greatest present problem, moreover — i.e. the ecology crisis in which all the contradictions of the prevailing mode of production and way of life, all the dangers of the world situation, intersect and coalesce — can by its very nature not be grasped at the level of the national state. True, the development of the productive forces, which by its dysfunctioning has precipitated a corresponding awareness of crisis, is related to national history, and a political practice that seeks its basis in this awareness cannot escape the traditions it strives to transform. Yet the challenge itself is non-specific, and at least a first account of it can be given that ignores national peculiarities, which in any case are more a question of practice than of theory.

All this may help to explain how it was that I did not feel too greatly surprised in West Germany. And another factor that helped me find my bearings was the way I was received by people of the most varied kind who sympathised with the concerns of *The Alternative in Eastern Europe*.[1] The difficulties of adaptation lie at a different and more subjective level, in the very different psychological atmosphere, the greater distance between people that social relations here impose.

Once I had decided to leave East Germany after my release from prison, I still had a year in Bautzen to prepare myself for the change. I learned a little French, considered the possibility of a deeper rapprochement between Marxism and Christianity, and above all I worked at a (lost) draft on the background and perspectives of the historic compromise. Should it not be possible to apply Berlinguer's initiative, suitably transformed, to conditions other than those of the Latin countries, especially of course those of West Germany? If this country is only half Catholic, and in a different way from Italy or Spain, then perhaps the experience of Scandinavian Eurocommunism and left socialism could more readily be turned to good use. I was already aware that the Scandinavian left had begun to intervene in the 'environmental movement', as it is known there.

The themes that inspired me in this connection are almost all tackled in the final section of the *Alternative*, or at least indicated — particularly in the chapter on 'The Present Conditions and Perspectives for General Emancipation'. I only needed to spin out these threads a little further. In this way, although all I knew of the Green movement in West Germany was that it existed, I came to a political conclusion in the form of a Left Socialist/Green joint list — i.e. an electoral alliance. Someone had told me that the Christian-Democrat member of parliament Herbert Gruhl had published a book on ecology and been expelled from his party, so that he was ready to join together with other forces who recognised the same danger. I took this right away as a symptom of a more widespread feeling, hence indicating the possibility of a new political combination.

The balance of political forces within West Germany, between right-wing conservatism and social reformism, certainly seemed to be basically fixed. There was scarcely any prospect of changing this unless one managed to reach over the Social-Democrat party and encroach on the support of the Christian-Democrats. The idea of a joint electoral list between the 'red Greens' hailing from the socialist left and the 'green Greens' concerned with the conservation of values [2] shows that I did not bank, from my distance, on a direct regroupment of these forces into a single body. This was why, in an interview with *Der Spiegel* immediately after my arrival, I said that the first set of forces, i.e. those socialists to the left of the SPD, had to find a unity among themselves [3] A few hours later Willy Brandt reminded me of his old experience with the Socialist Workers Party in the Weimar republic, and gave his opinion that the problem of little splinter groups would prove insoluble. We shall see, I thought, and I still think this now, though in a somewhat modified form.

In the meantime we have had the first Socialist Conference. [4] These forces need to find their productive role for the society as a whole, and must consequently undergo a fundamental change in their former mental and ideological constitution. I now believe that the way to achieve this is certainly not the establishment of a separate party turned in on itself. This would have difficulty in escaping from being a left splinter in the shadow of the Social-Democrats, it would remain tied to them by its very hostility. Nor would I favour the perspective that would probably ensue of competing on the terrain defined by the reformist hegemony with a 'better' trade-union policy. Above all, this would involve an endless struggle for a pure socialist programme. A left socialist party would be nothing more than an extension of the existing party spectrum, so long as it stood on the basis of this spectrum's completely outmoded structure. It would lead as a further consequence to a conservative ecology party coming into being, which would remain still more within the existing system. Last but not least, it would hinder the flow of discussion across existing party lines, something that is completely indispensable, especially (though not exclusively) vis-à-vis the Social-Democrats.

The ecology movement and the Green party are of such great importance for us because they act as a catalyst for a new political self-conception\and practice on the part of the left. The immediate impulse for my appearance at the preparatory congress of the Green party in Offenbach was given by Rudi Dutschke. At my press conference in Bonn the previous October [1979] he told me about the electoral success in Bremen.[5] The lesson of this was not to pursue the ecological cause through an external alliance between leftists and people from a conservative background, but rather as a kind of left faction within the Green party. This at least was how I understood him, but my understanding was wrong, for Dutschke precisely did not work in a factional way, and sharply distinguished himself from the effective obstruction of those comrades who sought to set themselves at the head of the new movement as a self-appointed vanguard of cadres.

The idea of a faction did not please me at all — initially at a purely emotional level — and I came to the conclusion that even the alliance I had in mind had the fatal undertone of a popular front: this always means just tactics, the lowest common denominator, rather than an ideological process and progress for both sides. To work as a faction would mean reproducing the traditional right-left pattern within the Green party (and unfortunately this is largely what has so far happened), seeking always to repel the other 'class line' in battles of votes. It would be hard for anything new to emerge from this, since it simply means that both sides throw each other back into their respective prejudices, into their own congealed past and limitations. What was to have been a common cause would thus remain largely at a distance. Communists have often made their allies fed up by this behaviour.

In November 1979 the first meeting took place between the 'green Greens' and the 'red Greens' of a certain spectrum. The atmosphere, however, was as bad as could be imagined. It was far worse than in the honeymoon periods of certain popular fronts. Chaos and division in Offenbach. In any case, no new popular front was emerging here. It rather seemed — though more as a farce than a serious drama — that the class struggle, which was not exactly raging elsewhere in society, was to take place at the conference of this newly forming party. It was precisely the left, and no one else, who continued this game from congress to congress — Karlsruhe, Saarbrücken, Dortmund — and almost rode the cause to death by constantly making the slogans of their own identification into questions of principle. For on the 'opposite' side it was only a small fringe of the spectrum represented who showed no readiness for compromise; many of them are far above us in patience and understanding. Anyone who is serious about a perspective with the Green party must be ready to overcome their past. If it is true that the East-West confrontation with its danger of war, the North-South conflict and the ecological crisis all overlap, what does this say for a project that seeks *as a preliminary* to deal finally with our particular national past, to fight the unresolved old struggles to an end? The problems to be settled have an objective relationship and rank order. If we do not manage in due time to bring together the forces required for a preventive transformation of our whole way of life, then resolutions that warn of a new fascist danger will in no way preserve us from the emergence of what they vaguely refer to, which is certainly not staved off by distancing oneself from the fascism of the past.

I am also unsure whether our anti-fascism — a way of attacking a generation whose fate we did not experience — protects us from being just as guilty as all those who 'knew nothing' at that time. The society in which we live is among other things the reason why between now and the end of the century at least 200 million people will die of hunger. Even though this still fails to get to the cause, we should for example — and starting with our own example — campaign for the people of the rich countries to reduce their consumption of meat and other animal products, since our agriculture costs far more calories in vegetable foodstuffs than it produces. In so far as our verbal radicalism inhibits the formation of a consensus around necessities of this kind, we can in no way wash our hands in innocence. The real yardstick should be adequate recognition of historical priorities and their implications for the way we deal with the society around us and with ourselves.

As can be seen from the Green movement, the ecology crisis is already affecting more people in their existential interests than is any other contradiction. The fact that its resolution is linked up with the struggle of other social interests, and the way that it is linked up, can become generally understood all the more quickly, the more intimate is the new context of discussion. Everyone who is basically committed will understand that social realities cannot be concealed. If the attempt were made to resolve the ecology crisis at the expense of those who already have a bad deal, then the increase in distress and the sharpening of struggles over distribution would precisely block the requisite steps being taken. It should be quite apparent to the overwhelming majority of those sensitive to the ecological cause that we need a breakthrough to greater social justice and security simply to make way for those fundamental changes without which there will be no future at all. The left, for its part, must understand that the perspective has shifted so radically that it has to take up quite different positions if it wants to successfully affect the parallelogram of forces. If it persists in its former coordinates and battle-lines, it could easily find itself a component part of the bloc that reproduces the existing situation.

Even the Green left is not immune from this danger. It was more than a tactical failure at the Dortmund congress when, even after an electoral platform that was acceptable to them had been passed, these people stood fast 'on the basis of the Saarbrücken programme' like a dog clinging to a hardly won bone, sought to promote their particular politics with counter-resolutions and withheld a place in the leadership from the most important representatives of the other wing. As long as we must still have these little victories, we show that we have not yet sufficiently internalised the key place of the ecological challenge. What is the value for us in the long run, and above all what is the value for the country, of a party to the left of the SPD with 2, 3 or 4 per cent of the vote? Are we seeking to march into a new impasse with this young alternative and protest movement, or rather to form an autonomous yet integrated component of the wider constructive forces that stand against the decomposition and self-destruction of our civilisation?

If we want to continue in the old way, we have to leave this business with the Greens alone. Let's not disturb them any more! Let them form a bourgeois ecology party, something that most of them don't even want. This would be consistent — consistent in the way of so many options of the left, with the end result that the balance of forces shifts against us and against change in general. But even people who have joined the ecology movement from the most bourgeois and conservative origins and mentality, or who are thinking of doing so, suspect that we have to transcend the capitalist horizon of the present economic order, and are ready to take up a new and different perspective. Their patience with the congresses of the Green party would otherwise be inexplicable. It is precisely due to what many people call their 'ecological one-sidedness' that they are far more ready than others to abandon something of their past. Do we or do we not have the same courage, the same ability?

Summer 1980

Our Forces Belong Together

Dear friends and comrades,

Having been invited here as a guest, I should like to present my attitude towards your cause. My attitude, nothing less, but also nothing more. You know that I have admitted being a 'closet' Green. And this means of course that I am now an 'out' Green.

Now Carl Amery, in making this diagnosis, was only able to refer to my *Alternative,* to the chapter on 'The Present Conditions and Perspectives for General Emancipation', on which the whole book turns. This is a socialist alternative, for the West as well as for the East. And that means Carl Amery[6] has indirectly established that a socialist position has produced what — at least in its intentions — is a comprehensive and radical Green approach, by which I still completely stand.

In any case, red and green, green and red, go well together.

The Greens already have their sights on more than just the ecological aspect. It is clear from all the literature I've seen that they stand for the general emancipation of human beings, men and women, and they want to overthrow all conditions in which people are debased and humiliated. But this was precisely the categorical imperative of the young Marx. General emancipation will never come about if we destroy the earth itself. And this destruction can only be prevented if we mobilise people on the basis of their most fundamental emancipatory impulses. Protest alone, mere opposition or resistance, is not enough. No programme can be based on throwing sand in the machine. We need a positive goal, for only then will be the remedy grow side by side with the danger. I am convinced, moreover, that discussion between socialists and ecologists, if conducted frankly and in public, will not lead to division but will bring together forces that belong together in history, and above all in any future perspective.

Our Freedom – the Freedom to Think Differently

In West Germany certain concepts such as 'communist' and even 'socialist' are tabooed in a way that is unparalleled elsewhere in Western Europe. Before all else, we socialists must ourselves understand correctly where the roots of this lie, and then act in such a way that we can again call ourselves unashamedly by our proper name. I have myself shown how and why it is that in Eastern Europe, as a result of the particular history of Russia and the Soviet Union, indeed of the entire non-capitalist world, there is a system that is called communist and calls itself socialist without in any sense being so. Anyone who seeks to improve conditions here in the Federal Republic must work to construct a new concept of socialism, one which will in fact be the original concept, stretching back to a German and West European Marx, who was moreover an unswerving internationalist. It stretches still further back, in fact, back to the broad spread of utopian socialists and communists of the 18th and 19th centuries, who stemmed largely from the bourgeois class and sought to turn the legacy of the Renaissance and the Enlightenment to serve the oppressed and underdeveloped of their own society.

We communists and socialists of today must cease calling the Soviet Union and Eastern Europe socialist or communist countries. The same naturally applies to China, for example.

If we do not, then we cannot but be misunderstood. Our goal is in no way an improved, purified version of this 'actually existing socialism'. It is a completely different system, as far removed from this 'actual socialism' as the Western world is. We cannot aim at anything that they have over there, with our two or three thousand years of West European civilisation behind us, from the ancient Greeks and the time of the *Iliad*. And we do not aim at anything like that, in no way whatsoever. To make this credible we must show by our actions that we are committed democrats, free of any hidden reservations. We must acknowledge and practise, in our own organisational principles, the freedom to think differently.

It is our responsibility to make this clear and to restore the great concept of socialism to the position it justly deserves, particularly in our country, Germany. After all, this is where Marx and Engels were born, and the philosophy of Marxism has its roots in the Tübingen seminary.[7] Democratic socialists and communists of all countries, moreover, have in the figure of Rosa Luxemburg, a woman who lived among us Germans until she was murdered, a human model who can today reunite us. We should be able to say to people: Look at this person, and you will see who we are and what we stand for.

It is clearer today than ever that the socialist attempt has so far been too narrowly based — even in its best form, where it has not been manipulated by a state bureaucracy. Today, socialism is and must be far more than a working-class and trade-union movement of the traditional kind. Otherwise the struggle for a just distribution of the social product between wage-earners and entrepreneurs in the rich industrial countries of the West will simply be fought on the backs of the rest of humanity. We can no longer behave as if the fate of us all depended on the outcome of domestic class struggles over wage levels, or on what party is dominant in the state. The tremendous contradictions on the North-South and East-West axes, which are inseparably bound together, overspill this context. This is something we cannot afford to forget, whether we define ourselves as socialists, as ecologists, or are seeking a concept that will bring these principles together. To pose the question purely in a domestic context — and in this sense Western Europe as a whole is still domestic politics — could only give rise to highly undesirable perspectives.

Negative Fixations and New Political Tasks

If it is permissible to quote Lenin, he was fond of the proverb that the biggest animal for the mouse is the cat. This reminds me a bit of the way in which the alternative forces in our country react to the established parties, for example, or to the question of nuclear power.

The established parties, indeed, permanently reject the demand of our time, which is to draw up a long-run policy for human survival and above all else to practise this. The question of nuclear power stations is simply one characteristic example of how our society deals in general with the question of technology. If it could be compelled to renounce a technology that is presently available, this would have a significance that could hardly be overrated.

But have we got our priorities right? For the danger of nuclear power stations, even if they are built, pales before the dangers in the wake of stationing a new generation of nuclear missiles in this country. If a new round of the arms race is set in motion — and this is quite evidently one of the most powerful driving forces of economic growth, waste of resources and environmental damage — then the movement against nuclear power could be like a dog barking round the legs of an elephant.

In this context, we must consider very responsibly the disposition of the political parties. Beyond the borders of our own country, whether vis-à-vis our Eastern partner and adversary, vis-à-vis Western Europe or in connection with a new North-South economic order, what actual difference does it make which of the two major parties, each of which is unsatisfactory, happens to head the government?

A movement that seeks to rescue a whole civilisation must be capable, sooner or later, of thinking its way out of the present overall interconnection. It must think on behalf of the totality. If a party to which we might formerly have belonged, or which we stood close to, has disappointed us, that is in itself no solution to the dilemma in which we are placed. The question of the Social-Democrat party is fundamentally the question of the balance of political-psychological forces in West Germany. We must be sufficiently far-sighted in determination and in ideas to change this balance of forces. Then we shall perhaps change the SPD as well. But can we hope to achieve any really significant results without the forces that this party represents? I believe such a strategy could lead at best to a Pyrrhic victory, precisely for the purest of ecological motivations. Critical and effective challenge to the social-reformist tendency is necessary; confrontation with it based on resentment would be disastrous.

For the time being, we should at least leave as much as possible open. For all the reduction of real differences in government policy and administrative practice, it is not true, in terms of future perspective, that both cats are equally grey. We should not forget the experience of Weimar, and what happened when the German Communists of that time believed they should concentrate their attack on the Social-Democrats, since these were the main prop of the bourgeoisie and hence even worse than the bourgeoisie itself.

Our West European civilisation, both here and in those other parts of the globe where it has taken root, cannot be saved and reconciled with other civilisations unless a broad concentration of political forces comes into being, mobilising the power of the masses to change our overall direction. To me this concentration seems inconceivable without the various forces of the socialist tradition standing at the centre of such a bloc. For we shall not succeed in forcing our way through any ecological bottleneck, or bringing to a halt what is called economic growth, unless we first manage to bring under rigorous control the *economic mechanism* of monopoly competition for maximum profits, rising sales and market shares — all ultimately one and the same — and proceed to replace this completely as the regulatory mechanism. And as for the alienated structure of people's needs which is so important to overcome from the Green standpoint too, subjectively perhaps the most important thing — is this not above all else the reverse side of that same economic principle?

The psychological revolution that we all see as urgently needed is precisely directed against the mode of consumption created by capitalism. It cannot be broken if we leave the economic motor untouched.

All concrete measures that the ecological project proposes count in fact on a transformation effected via the state, from the municipal level, through the provincial level, up to the national and international levels. We must develop a policy for transforming the state machine, over the long term, into an instrument of social control over all the special monopoly interests. This requires a mass movement, but a movement that will encompass the whole range of forces who can be made sensitive to these problems, and that will drive a wedge between the state apparatus, which itself consists of human beings, and the monopoly lobbies of all kinds. Then the state apparatus can function in a new direction, one prescribed to it by the interests of the majority.

The Forces that Must Come Together

To summarise:

the socialists need the Greens, for survival is the precondition for them to attain their traditional goals;

the Greens need the socialists, for survival can only be ensured by disconnecting the motor of monopoly competition.

We must now go on to expand the political-psychological context in a further very basic dimension. We must appeal to all people of good will who have a stake in the fundamental premises of our civilisation and want to preserve and carry forward its values. What I have in mind here are the liberal traditions, and above all committed Christians.

The Christians need the socialists. I have written how capitalism is the epoch furthest from God.[8] Christians, even entire churches, are now taking a stand on all the really key questions for the fate of our civilisation, opposing themselves to the effects of the prevailing economic system. But a moral appeal is ineffective without political action. We must prepare the political context for this.

We socialists, in turn, need the Christians. Because of our traditional task of representing the underprivileged masses, we find it hard to abandon the accumulation of material well-being in favour of other, more subjective, values. We must open our ears to the precept 'Do not store up treasures on earth'. Here today, in countries as rich as ours, the true sense of the New Testament is once again as clear as day. It was not to the poor that Christ preached poverty, not to the humiliated and oppressed that he preached humility, nor to the shy wallflowers that he preached modesty in enjoyment. Our experience of prosperity has brought home to us once again how the need for some kind of religious transcendence is a disposition of human nature, of our spiritual world, i.e. a mental reality. Marxists, too, should take note of this.

Moreover, whenever a real cultural transformation has taken place in history, this has never been without a mobilisation that has stretched right into this most intimate sphere of human motivation. In our own civilisation Christ was incontestably the first teacher of our ultimate goal, the first teacher of the general emancipation of humanity.

In short, we must seek to bring into one single movement all the forces that strive in the direction of our goal, that of rescuing our civilisation and world civilisation in general, and bringing about the general emancipation of human beings — men and women. We must throw out all dogmatic ballast that prevents such unification. Nothing could stand more in the way than traditional left sectarianism, or any other kind. Anyone is welcome to cultivate their favourite theoretical ideas, their particular way in to the common cause, and thus make a positive contribution. But they should not make this an obstacle for others.

We must offer responsible people in all three established parties — people who still aspire to something more than the daily round of political arithmetic and administration and who in no way need all follow us equally visibly — the prop of an ideal, as a means of regeneration. Mere negation and rejection is no programme here, but can only lead to a sham-revolutionary subjectivism.

There was never a time when people were so united as they are now on the existence of the problems which humanity is presently faced with. Should we not assist people of different views to converge together in whatever way is appropriate?

It seems to me that we should consider at greater length and in more detail the formulation of our goal and the way of linking up into a movement that can transform our country, which is still a thing of beauty, starting from within. We should develop our programme in such a way that it contains, in embryo, the possibility of winning a majority in the long run.

Today we may well have here the authentic and potentially successful beginnings of a mass movement of cultural transformation. So as not to endanger it by short-sighted adventures, we should not be too hasty in fixing our definitions. We must take the time needed to arrive at a distinct project, together with the majority of those already participating in the movement and a far wider constituency as well, a project that is oriented not just to the community, local and provincial levels, but to the national and international levels too, and can seize opportunities at all these levels. Then what has started out on a small scale at the grass roots, and from the midst of our existential problems, can develop into something very big; it has now to come together on a broader basis.

Speech at the Offenbach congress, November 1979

Ecology Crisis and Socialist Idea

In the industrially developed countries today there is scarcely any subject that so urgently needs to be tackled as that of 'the socialist alternative and ecology', at least no more important subject for socialists and no more important subject for ecologists or Greens. Socialists and Greens — and by Greens here I mean especially those who are not also socialists, for indeed many of us socialists are also Greens — can discuss this subject on a very favourable reciprocal basis. They have long had a certain standpoint in common, which has now become decisive for world history. This common standpoint is a radical critique of capitalist industrialism. Many Greens may initially think not of capitalist industrialism but of the consequences of the industrial system in general. But in this respect they are misled. This is easy for them to see if they look back in history and ask when the basic attitudes they proceed from first came into being. They will find that these attitudes, which now govern their critique from the ecological standpoint, took shape in the early Romantic era, about 200 years ago. More than once, for example, Herbert Gruhl in his book *A Planet is Plundered* refers precisely to this period of the last 200 years, in which our mode of production and life has developed in the direction of the catastrophe that we now see on the horizon. But this is not just industry in general — for the ancient Chinese already had industry, so too the Greeks to a certain degree — but industry on a capitalist basis, industry that is driven on by the boundless need to valorise capital, to make value into more value; this development set in around the middle of the 18th century. European development in the last 200 years is the development of industry on this capitalist basis. This is a connection which no one concerned with the Green movement can overlook.

The Romantic critique of capitalism was originally applied to the consequences of this specific form of industrialisation on human beings. This was right from the start an anti-capitalist critique. All industry that has spread across the planet from the English industrial revolution through to today is capitalist industry — in its technical structure, its technology, its type of jobs and work organisation. For even where non-capitalist relations obtain, the principles of science and technology are imported from Europe, North America and Japan. The entire Green critique of the existing economic order is directed — whether deliberately or not, avowedly or not — at the mechanism that has effected the tremendous technical and scientific progress in Europe since the first industrial revolution. We socialists can and must offer those Greens who are at the moment not socialists our detailed explanation of the connection between capitalist expanded reproduction on the one hand and the anarchic industrial growth, a technology that is alien and hostile to human beings, on the other, and we must do this comprehensively and quite patiently.

We must also explain to them in concrete terms, if mutual trust is to develop, why we failed to discover sooner what is now a common basis as far as our anti-capitalist critique of industry is concerned. Other political forces, concerned that traditional conservatives and communists — to name the extremes — should not meet in the Green movement, remind us socialists that only yesterday we attacked the attitude now expressed, for example, in Gruhl's book, as a conservative or even Romantic and reactionary critique of capitalism. And they are quite right. The socialist and workers' movement did indeed see its rise and the perspective of its final victory as bound up with the growth of capitalist industry, so that it criticised the capitalist character of this industry from a 'more advanced' rather than a backward-looking point of view. How basically justified they were to do so is shown by the advantages that not only the capitalists but also the working masses in the developed countries have received from industrialisation — for all the distorted effects. Certainly no one will deny this. The hymn to the bourgeoisie Marx sings in the *Communist Manifesto* before he condemns capitalism, this critical praise for the production of wealth that is the precondition for the free development of all members of society, remains true.

But today we have reasons for restricting our rejection of Romantic anti-capitalism, if not abandoning it altogether. And here I intend to develop these reasons.

First of all, in the meantime capitalism has fulfilled its task of creating wealth through the advance of industry as the basis for general human emancipation, as far as countries such as this are concerned; indeed it may have over-fulfilled this task. To speak of average income, i.e. the sum of produced values that someone can buy here for this income, people have on average more than was needed in the 18th century, or even in the 19th, in order to produce a fully developed human being. If this effect has not materialised, it is not for want of means of subsistence — with the exception of some not very large marginal groups. And no matter how unjust the present distribution from the standpoint of internal class contradictions, there is no reason to suspect that further increases in real income will suffice to make people more cultivated and happy. What we have is rather a social order in which obvious gains in comfort and time for the individual — whether a worker, an employee, an official, an intellectual, or whatever — bring hardly any gain in human freedom and dignity.

If we imagine the abolition of capitalism, which enforces such a wasteful consumption pattern, we can see that we do not need more material goods in this country, at least not from the usual spectrum of products. On the contrary, in many respects we already have too many. To put it a different way, it is only because capitalism exists, because our industry is still pursued capitalistically and the proceeds are inequitably distributed, that the working people in the rich countries still have a relative need for rising real incomes. Thus so long as those Greens who are not yet socialists address their critique of growth primarily to capitalism, they will certainly have the right to make a general call for restraint, directed in the second place also at working people. What matters is the recognition that capitalism must be done away with.

We socialists need to consider how the restraint policies of the monopolies and the state can be countered by a restraint policy developed from the standpoint of the majority of the population. We cannot tell the peoples of the Southern half of the planet that all exploitation and oppression, all want and starvation is the fault of our capitalists. As of now, we socialists are living in this bourgeois society, so are our workers, and the trade unions are struggling within it too; we all share in the profits from colonialism and neo-colonialism. Ultimately we also share responsibility for the fact that our society is still a bourgeois society, and that we have still not altered or overcome capitalism.

My comrades on the far left — though perhaps we should gradually do away with this right-left diagram from bourgeois parliamentarism — like to ask at this point whether the decisive thing, if capitalism is finally to disappear, isn't to organise the class struggle of the proletariat. And if you reply by asking them how long we are to continue banking on this proletarian revolution, as we have already done for a long time in vain, they answer that you have to be patient and rely on the fact that the objective class interest of the workers will win through in the end. I do not want to discuss here how questionable this 'objective class interest' is even in the traditional Marxist view — that would mean bringing in a lot of other new points. One thing however seems quite clear to me: We cannot make the rest of humanity, or ourselves, wait patiently any longer for this promised proletarian general solution; there is simply no time left. Who will guarantee a general solution by the year 2000?

Just examine the projections for materials and energy consumption for the next few decades, as well as those for environmental damage, and consider what would happen if the peoples of the rest of the world were to follow the example set by our civilisation here. (Ultimately everyone must have the right to live in the same way and 'as well' as we do, if we define our life here and now as a good one.) Under these circumstances we should have to multiply our present consumption of energy and raw materials by ten, and — since our own consumption is clearly still growing, and will continue to do so — by more than ten. It is high time indeed to realise that we cannot and must not go on in this way — quite irrespective of whether capitalism is going to last or whether we are able to overcome it as quickly as we hope. In as much as we take ourselves seriously as Marxists and socialists, this means that we have to examine and improve our entire mental equipment. We have to adapt it to a changed and fundamentally expanded main task for the socialist movement.

Our customary idea of the transition to socialism is the abolition of the capitalist order within the basic conditions European civilisation has created in the field of technique and technology — and not in Europe alone. Even in this century, a thinker as profound as Antonio Gramsci was still able to view technique, industrialism, Americanism, the Ford system in its existing form as by and large an inescapable necessity,and thus depict socialism as the genuine executor of human adaptation to modern machinery and technology. Marxists have so far rarely considered that humanity has not only to transform its relations of production, but must also fundamentally transform the entire character of its mode of production, i.e. the productive forces, the so-called technostructure. It must not see its perspective as bound up with any historically transmitted form of the development of needs and their satisfaction, or of the world of products designed for this purpose. The commodity world that we find around us is not in its present form a necessary condition of human existence. It does not have to look the way it does in order for human beings to develop both intellectually and emotionally as far as we would like.

The type of expanded reproduction that European civilisation brought about in its capitalist era, this avalanche-like increasing expansion in all dimensions of material technique, is beginning to prove unsustainable — economically, politically and psychologically. The success we have had with our means of dominating nature threatens to annihilate both ourselves and everyone else it draws mercilessly into its wake. The present way of life of the most industrially advanced nations stands in a global and antagonistic contradiction to the natural conditions of human existence. We are eating up what other nations and future generations need to live on. At the very least, our waste of all easily accessible resources is increasing their necessary labour and thus preventing their liberation from the traditional historical constraints.

Governed by the economic principle of surplus-value production and profit maximisation this is an essentially quantitative process, and scarcely convertible into human gain. Hegel used to speak in such cases of a 'bad infinity', by which he meant a process which involved no more than adding 1 to 1, and did not lead in its own context to a decisive qualitative leap. This kind of progress must cease, for the share of the earth's crust that can be ground up in the industrial metabolism is limited, despite all possible and senseless expansion, if the planet is to remain habitable.

The technocratic and scientist faith that the progress of industry, science and technique will solve humanity's social problems virtually automatically is one of the illusions of the present age most hostile to life. The so-called scientific and technical revolution that is still moving ahead chiefly in this dangerous perspective must be reprogrammed by a social transformation. The very idea of progress must be interpreted in a completely new way. The per capita consumption of raw materials and energy, the per capita production of steel and cement that are adduced in all the statistics as criteria of progress, are typical criteria of a progress that is totally alienated.

This battle for production, by its innermost mechanisms, fails to lead us out of the balance of terror that all generals celebrate, or out of the shortage of means of subsistence and personal development. 'The realm of natural necessity, since that of needs' is expanding with no foreseeable limit, in a direction different from that which Marx had in mind. For the more needs people develop in this senseless direction, the longer they must work, and the less time remains for free human self-development and fulfilment. Inevitably, we are steadily pushing back the historical moment 'at which compulsion and the monopolisation of social development (with its material and intellectual advantages) by one section of society at the expense of another disappears'.[9] The rise in labour productivity supposed to serve the goal of increasing the time available for individual development has been perverted into a vehicle of this ominous race to consume ever more raw materials.

Apart therefore from the need of the developing countries to catch up, which will hopefully not be measured by our present standards, it is not true that we need this economic growth for generations to come. It is already facing humanity with ever more problems than it is able to solve, given the existing social structure, with the aid of science, technique and organisation. All too often Beelzebub is used to drive out the devil. The policy of growth proves rather to be a stabilising agency for the present relations of domination, both here and in the other bloc as well.

The communist association in Marx's sense of the word, which has nothing in common with what is to be seen in the states of 'actually existing socialism', was to be a social body that is master of its problems without suffocating the individuals who comprise it. Marx himself, moreover, had the idea that modern communism would have something in common with the primitive community, a communism of solidarity and simple reproduction of the conditions of life. This is being confirmed today. We can see how such an association of free individuals can only be an order of quantitatively simple reproduction of human beings, instruments and material goods, or at least a very slow and measured expansion. This is true in the last instance for the planet as a whole. It is necessary to resolve the problem of the tremendous differences in living standard as quickly as possible, instead of opening these scissors still wider. Only in this way can the relative surplus of the necessities of life that Marx declared a condition for socialist and communist relations come into being on a world scale. Given the continuing sway of the old economic system with its permanent 'revolution in expectations' driven forward by the latest needs for luxury, this relative surplus can never be attained.

Marx in his time had particularly in mind means of subsistence in the strict sense, those things that are necessities of life for everyone. In the industrialised countries the driving dialectic of production and need has shifted onto the field of means of enjoyment and personal development, yet the manipulation of needs conditioned by capital has seriously deformed the supply of goods for both enjoyment and development alike, i.e. for the appropriation of culture. It is not the case, in other words, that we have these means of enjoyment and development in the form in which they genuinely do serve rational human enjoyment and the higher development of the individual. We find them in a form that is largely perverted. Many needs that point to particular means of enjoyment and development, or should do so, have a merely compensatory character, i.e. they aim at a substitute satisfaction for a development of the personality that is lacking, being inhibited by existing conditions. What is bought often blocks the mental progress of the purchaser instead of promoting this. The compensatory desire and need to have, to spend and to consume consequently force the continuation of the capitalist battle for production, meaning that even in a hundred years we shall still be 'too poor' for socialism. It will always be possible to say that something is lacking, because someone else has a bit more. The vicious circle of the capitalist growth dynamic must be broken, precisely from the standpoint of the socialist interest in human emancipation.

Besides, it is only with a slow evolution of technology that a reliable self-regulation of the social process can gradually come into being, which would be the opposite of control by a bureaucratic mechanism. With the present tempo of technical and technological evolution, a repressive state is unavoidable. Bureaucracy is the inescapable consequence of the spontaneity with which the laws of our fetishised world of objects rule over us. As long as necessary labour continues to harrass people, as long as more and more objectified labour is 'necessary' to satisfy a person's needs, there can be no end to the struggle to obtain what is needed, no end to the bourgeois principle of equal right for unequal individuals, and no end to the state.

In order to become master of nature, humanity had to reproduce itself and its tools on an expanded scale. This was at one time a progressive necessity. But in order to remain in nature and to gain control over itself, humanity must stabilise itself in its relationship with nature. For the young Marx, the abolition of private property in the means of production was precisely to bring about the reconciliation of culture and nature. Marx already perceived the contradiction between capitalist production and nature. It was just that this was as yet not so acute for him to place it at the centre of his analysis. Later on this point of view retreated more to the margin of Marx's thinking, since he concentrated closely on analysing the capital relationship in the stricter sense, i.e. on the problems that at that time stood most in the way of the further development of working humanity. The idea of a communist society as what Marx called a true resolution of the conflict between humanity and nature as well as the conflict between human beings, in no way became lost; not even the idea of abolishing the conflict between humanity and its own nature, its own physiology and psychology, which is also a part of nature (and in present conditions often an unmastered part). It is possible to imagine, then, how Marx would have developed his ideas if he had had the opportunity of thinking through the contradiction between humanity and nature in its present dimensions.

The extensive phase of humanity is approaching its end, for better or for worse. The species can and will continue to improve its material base, but it has to break with the lunatic worship of size, for the sake of its continued existence and also for the sake of giving meaning to its life; it has to learn to pay collective attention to its relationship with nature. I would even use the word 'humility' in this connection. Up to now our species has been more accustomed to upsetting its natural context than to improving it. Science has always proceeded further with its encroachments than its knowledge of the ensuing implications has extended. The leap into the realm of freedom is conceivable only against the background of a balance between human nature and the environment, the dynamic of this balance being shifted towards the qualitative and subjective. Here in the rich countries we are the first to face the task of attempting this breakthrough. If we do not succeed in organising society in such a way that it can follow this direction in time, it will very soon be forced to do so under the blows of catastrophic collapses in civilisation, marked by barbaric struggles and dictatorships. There is still time.

The Difficulty of Changing the World

We must now take into account the fact that existing conditions have penetrated deep into people's habits. Gorki once said of the difficulty in changing the world that the basic theme of all moans and groans on the part of the majority was: 'Don't stop us living as we are used to', and I would add: 'Don't stop us expanding as we are used to'. Our social life is organised in such a way, both here and in the other bloc, that even people who work with their hands are more interested in a better car than in the single meal of the slum-dweller on the Southern half of the earth or the need of the peasant there for water; even a concern to expand their own consciousness, for their own self-realisation, takes second place. There is however a surplus of consciousness today that is greater than ever before. This simply means that there is, as it were, sufficient free time for the development of the forces of both head and heart. People here need no longer be totally absorbed by work that they cannot use for their own development. True, these portions of development time are still quite inequitably distributed in our own country, and this continues to form the major and justified point of attack of the workers' and trade-union movement. Not least, the distribution is also one prejudicial to women, and this must also be changed. The capacities for it are to hand.

We know that alienated labour and the pressure of the prevailing institutions *initially* determine the mass of this surplus consciousness, this free capacity in the sense of free time, in such a way that people use this free time to strive for comfortable substitute satisfactions, for instance on the lines of the many illustrated magazines which always show the same thing. Conditions restrict and obstruct the development, fulfilment and self-affirmation of countless people from their earliest youth onwards. And they are often forced to seek compensation in the consumption of things, in passive entertainment, in attitudes oriented to prestige and power. These are the compensatory interests I have already mentioned, for which individuals taken together cannot be made directly responsible, but which must be put down in the last instance to the prevailing mechanism of reproduction in our society, i.e. ultimately to economic relations. In so far as the ecology crisis forces us — as socialists — to deal with the problem of these compensatory needs, the problem of how they are to be mastered, it indirectly also offers a positive opportunity for our traditional socialist ideals, with which we have got into an impasse in the course of the last few decades. The transition to a new overall type of economic reproduction is required not only on account of the crisis of environment and resources, but also in order to relax the impulse to strive for substitute satisfactions.

As I have said, the competition for growth enforces inequality in material living standards between individuals and nations, and hence enforces these substitute satisfactions. The more is produced — and this is precisely how the capitalist market mechanism functions — the more must be pursued, possessed, displayed and consumed, the more mental energy is tied to abstract labour and compensatory enjoyments and remains withdrawn from the emancipatory forces. The material insatiability that capitalism trains us in costs us the freedom of higher development and subjects us once more to regulations that rest on compulsion. If the explosion of material needs caused by the hunt for profit and the widening of markets cannot be brought to a halt, then socialism will not only be economically impossible, but psychologically impossible as well. This is why we socialists have such a great interest in the ecology movement — also in the interest of our own original goals.

From Emancipation in Economics to Emancipation from Economics

Many people, taken individually, suspect that the idea of progress must today be conceived in a completely new and original way. Scarcely anyone — contrary to what it may sometimes seem — is really absorbed completely in these compensatory satisfactions, once their necessities of life are secured. It is the prevailing economic relations and the institutions pertaining to them which prevent people from drawing the conclusions and living according to their better insights and desires. Because of this, and not as it were the other way round, these better insights and desires cannot develop fully at first. They have to develop against the tide, and this is precisely where the need arises for a union of these opposing forces, from which the individual can draw support. An alternative, emancipatory organisation against the prevailing organisations which absorb and manipulate people! This is on the agenda today. It means a grand alliance of all forces and tendencies which seek to extricate people from the confinement of material constraints which they have themselves created, but which are ultimately determined from outside. It was precisely in this sense that I spoke in Offenbach of the need for a close alliance with the Christians.[10] Today the question is not just one of emancipation in economics, but a perspective at least of emancipation from economics, of rising above the realm of necessity, as Marx considered it.

What is needed is to completely reprogramme the whole of economic life, the entire relationship of production and need as well as the regulation of the economic process. Without this there can be no human emancipation — an emancipation that involves the individual, otherwise it's not emancipation at all. The psychological dimension of the problem of individuality in super-complex industrial society must be made completely clear. The different spheres of life — work, education, housing, recreation — are so separated from one another, almost all activities are so depersonalised and even private ties stripped of so many necessities, that the alienation of one person from another threatens to become the general fate. The misfortune of loneliness, of total loss of communication beneath the gigantic surface of abstract, spiritually indifferent functional activities, bites ever deeper. We find a loss of emotional connection even in the intimate contacts of the nuclear family, this last residue of the original community. A mode of life that leads to such disharmony for individuals may be progressive according to some criterion or other, but it is devoid of any perspective of human emancipation.

If the question is raised as to where the real causes of this process lie, it would most likely prove very superficial to attribute them to the last ten years of the socialist-liberal coalition, for example. Behind this result lies those 200 years of development of our present civilisation, which has essentially been determined by capitalism.

Increases in production and productivity, which are very seldom critically examined, must lose their present halo of inescapable economic requirements, which does not mean we should necessarily erect 'zero growth' in the quantitative sense into an economic law. The real question is not whether to have zero growth or 5 per cent growth or 2 per cent. That is not the point at all. The point is that we have to escape from the law that mere quantity rules. And quantity rules simply as a function of the underlying economic principle, the money principle, this principle of capitalism, where the question is always just how to make one mark into two. This is the quantity principle that drives our economic order. And we have to put an end to this quantity principle so that growth can take a qualitative turn, a turn into the subjective.

If a society is sufficiently industrialised that it can more or less reliably satisfy the elementary needs of its members at the level of civilisation that has been reached, the whole process of reproduction must then be gradually but deliberately transformed — and this means in a planned way, planning of this kind is unavoidable — to give priority to all-round human development, to an increase in the positive possibilities of human happiness. In the last analysis, the ever spreading individual discontent in our present civilisation has long signalled a contradiction of such magnitude as to make our present way of life unsustainable even if the decline or impoverishment of resources did not set any limits to material expansion. Historical examples, moreover, show that the same or similar results of human development and happiness are possible even with a fairly great difference in the quantity of available products. In no case can the conditions of freedom be given in dollars or roubles per head.

The people of the developed countries do not need to expand their present needs, they need rather the opportunity to enjoy themselves in their own individualised activities: the enjoyment of doing things, the enjoyment of friendship, concrete life in the widest sense — the sense that Goethe's Faust sought to live and prefigure. This is the real task that today faces every human being, and no longer just the privileged bourgeois who stood at the centre of Goethe's world stage. We need a new overall plan for social development oriented to new values, a plan which the economy has naturally to fit into. A plan geared to the optimisation of conditions of development for fully socialised human beings. This means, for example, priority for expenditure on education, it means educational planning that is no longer governed by the present state of demand for material values, or by what jobs industry has to offer. And we need the planning to be done in forms of grass-roots democracy that facilitate a process of social learning and discovery with the broadest mass participation. We need a social planning process which lays down new value orientations for the entire apparatus of production to pursue. A plan of this kind need not be just the activity of a state machine, but can be an activity undertaken simultaneously from above and from below, if there is a genuine mass communication about these value orientations and goals.

On the Anti-Fascist Potential of an Ecological Politics

Against the background I have just developed, I thus believe that on very many points we socialists today agree — even if proceeding from a different motivation — with those standpoints of radical critique of technique and technology, industry, etc. which we used to reject as conservative, petty-bourgeois, feudal-socialist, etc. We must just always add, to paraphrase Cato in ancient Rome: capitalism must be destroyed. On this question of the critique of industry and technology we find ourselves aligned with conservative positions that are fed from a different tradition — and we can and must and should align ourselves with these.

Our standpoint is that a radical critique of capitalist industrialism can provide the common basis on which we can work together in the Green movement across the whole spectrum of forces interested in overcoming our present crisis of civilisation. Anti-capitalist, of course, doesn't immediately mean the same as socialist. We are well aware of this, and do not imagine we can right away confirm these anti-capitalist tendencies as socialist. We just want to bring our own standpoints into the discussion, the perspective I have sought to develop here. In this way we shall have a broad common denominator of criticism of capitalist industrialism even where the problem of capitalism is not understood right from the start. And in this perspective I agree to a large extent with Herbert Gruhl's formulation: neither to the right nor to the left in the traditional sense (at least not far to the left), but ahead.

A changed attitude towards conservative motivations, moreover, such as is suggested by the ecology crisis, will have a considerable anti-fascist importance. There are comrades and friends who on the one hand point to the danger of Franz-Josef Strauss and warn — pointlessly, because inexactly — of a new 1933, while on the other hand they discover among the Greens ideological elements which in a previous age were taken up and exploited by the Nazis. With arguments of this kind they back up their thesis that 'the Greens are helping Strauss', which otherwise is based simply on electoral arithmetic. I would say that these comrades and friends are themselves helping Strauss with arguments such as this, and moreover at a far more fundamental level than that of arithmetic. They say to those Greens who are not socialists and proceed from a conservative motivation that they should go back where they came from, or are coming from. And they remind those many people who are still completely trapped in conservative values that they should remain with the reactionary major political party of monopoly capital, whose adherence to traditional and Christian values is purely demagogic.

They fail to understand that we have the duty and the task of helping to provide people like this with a better political home. They fail to understand that we ourselves shared responsibility, with our too rationalistic conception of class interests and their translation into political action, for the fact that so many people fell helpless prey to fascist demagogy in the past — a demagogy which in no way corresponded to their true interests and intentions. It was not the peasant with entailed land who gave rise to fascism, for example, but rather fascism that made these peasants into a reactionary symbol. Instead of conjuring up the old fascism of 1933, we should concern ourselves chiefly with how we can undermine the Strauss party, how we can draw people away from it, as we are in a historical position to do. To a large degree, reactionaries speculate on the same frustrations that worry us. What irritates us socialists about them is often no more than the different guise, the different terminology. We must be ready for dialogue, and permit ourselves concepts which we are not accustomed to and which do not stem from our own school.

To summarise this train of thought, there is today no better long-run anti-fascist guarantee in this country than a well-founded alliance, intellectual and emotional, of socialists and ecologists in a growing Green movement. A Green movement that does not just support against Strauss a Social-Democrat party which is purely on the defence and devoid of ideas for the future, but — in the long term — could change this party's own mentality. What this needs is an Archimedian point outside of the SPD, which has sold out to the business of government. Of course this Green movement is far broader than the Green party as this will be formed. But precisely because the Green movement is broader than a political party, all socialists both within and outside the SPD have a common responsibility towards this movement, a responsibility for comradely collaboration.

The Difference Between Independence and Sectarianism

When I say 'all socialists', I naturally include the comrades of the Communist groups, leagues and parties who also have a great opportunity, in connection with the Green movement, of emerging from the offside left, from trading in mere formulas, from fixation on foreign models that are unrealisable in our part of the world. It seems to me that these organisations do not need to abandon their status, but rather to define it in a new way. If the comrades intend to join the Green party, they can naturally not continue to belong to organisations which maintain the same claim to party status, i.e. want to take part in elections at the level of a political party. Nor should it surprise us that the Social-Democrats insist on the incompatibility between SPD and Green membership. There is nothing remarkable in this. (What is remarkable is only that the SPD has so swiftly decided on something that is so obvious, that it sees it as necessary to beat against thin air.) Does this mean that existing organisations should be dissolved overnight? Certainly not. A normal political party in a pluralist society has room for many tendencies. And these tendencies must have the right to organise their own discussion, to maintain a certain cohesion (and why not therefore under the banner of a Communist League?) in order to elaborate their particular concerns and also publish their own literature. The point is that we should organise our work as socialists, as communists, at the ideological level; and not at the level of those organisations who want to administer and command their members and keep entangling people who join them in conflicts of loyalty when any new developments begin. I have had enough of this. If people want to maintain more than a discussion organisation concerned with a particular standpoint and the constructive application of this, if they want their own Leninist party discipline — which in conditions here means the discipline of a sect — then there will of course always be quarrels, and comrades who still stick to this model will lose their chance of escaping from isolation.

As far as the Green, Multicoloured and Alternative[11] lists are concerned, there should be an end to division. What is emerging is a single movement. Green is as good a name for this as any other. The Green label will obviously prevail, it obviously has prevailed already. Green means ecological, and this is indeed the most important point of view. And since the Green movement sees itself as also meaning grass-roots democracy, since it sees itself also as 'social' (much as this concept needs further precision) and non-violent — it will already be Multicoloured in many respects, indeed it is already Multicoloured. And it will be Alternative in the broadest sense of a constructive opposition to the politics and practices of the established parties.

This means that it will provide room for the whole spectrum of interests which are provoked to resistance by the existing order of things. It will provide room for those comrades who have up to now been split off in the Communist groups, and who should join it and work together in it without having to jettison their own ideological organisation. We must free ourselves from the psychology of reciprocal contamination, of treating the problem of Green/Multicoloured/Alternative/Communist groups in a way that is precisely not alternative but displays a typical kind of wheeling and dealing.

We must be ready for a while, in a spirit of generosity, to put up with certain reactions which have arisen possibly in response to our own sectarianism as well as from the general anti-communist prejudice. We have to be well aware of the background against which these came about. And we have ourselves the greatest responsibility for dealing with these prejudices in a positive manner, undermining them by our own behaviour. In view of the great social necessity of a convergent Green movement, conscious socialists should in no way make a fuss about immediately getting our fair share, being adequately represented on this or that electoral list. The old slogan that we have nothing to lose but our chains is very applicable here. We should ask ourselves what we actually possess apart from our tiny organisational cohesion. What do we possess in the way of actual influence on society beyond our own circles, and what influence might we have if we joined in without sectarianism? And when this is examined, the answer is that we really do have nothing to lose but our chains. For what we have in our heads in the way of a particular understanding gained from our socialist attitude, what we can thus continue to develop and must daily compare with the outside world, is something that no one can or wants to take away.

The Greens, for their part, in as much as they might want to exclude former Multicoloured and Alternative people, should not forget the kind of process that is involved in abandoning sectarianism. (Since I arrived in this country I have myself been warned of sectarianism more than I have encountered it: I should at least make this clear. And by whom? By comrades in the SPD, for example.) There is a process of self-understanding under way of great breadth and depth. This takes time. And those Greens who are still not socialists should also bear this in mind.

A degree of openness and generosity (an alternative degree, I might say) should moreover be displayed on all sides, and we especially need a discussion as to which goals should be given priority in the movement. For instance, it is still not ecological enough, the ecological approach itself is still conceived in too narrow a fashion.

From Internal to Global Contradictions

Against the background of the general points I made at the beginning, which emphasised more the particular kind of interest that ties us socialists to the ecology movement and where the mutual connection lies, I now want to deal once more with the ecological crisis itself. We are still not sufficiently clear how few minutes to midnight it is — in terms of the whole of human history to date.

What we now face is a crisis of human civilisation in general. There has never been anything comparable in the whole past history of our species on this earth. All previous struggles were local in character, and however inadmissible any numerical comparison of greater and lesser numbers of victims, in previous times there was always a future surrounding the contending parties, new and unspent forces outside the field of battle. It was thus possible for clans, tribes, city states, empires to fight one another in what was at least in part still a real struggle for survival in the sense of biological evolution. The Thirty Years War 'only' destroyed Germany, the First World War 'only' Central Europe, the Second World War 'only' destroyed, devastated and depopulated Europe, even though it also spread to include North Africa and East Asia. The situation could arise — and Marx and Engels always saw this as a possibility — that the adversaries in an internal class struggles might completely obliterate one another, knocking all the pieces off the board until the two kings were left in a mutual stalemate. On other boards other struggles would have more fortunate results. The life and death of the entire social body was not a question that arose everywhere simultaneously.

Today there is either 'one world or none', in the title of a book by Ossip K. Flechtheim. Humanity has a single destiny. When I was in prison I read the Bible right through for the first time. Previously I was only acquainted with part of it. Now I remain as before a socialist and a Marxist. I did not read it as a work of edification, but because it is necessary for us to come to terms and debate with this spiritual achievement, this great humanist tradition. So I am going to take an example from the Bible in order to characterise our present situation.

The prophet Isaiah feared for his people, and prayed and struggled with his God that, even if a historical catastrophe should occur, the number of those spared should be as large as possible. We should recognise that today we have come quite close to this tragic situation in which Isaiah stood — and this applies to the people of every continent, of every colour of skin and every social class and stratum on this one earth, as a single people. If what is going on now continues for a further twenty, thirty, forty or fifty years, then our earth will be stripped bare. We shall be like a swarm of locusts who multiply and fall upon a certain territory, eat it bare and then all perish themselves. This tendency is now an acute one in world history, since our planet is indeed limited and the development of our species exhibits precisely this locust-like phenomenon — not only as far as its numbers are concerned, but also in terms of consumption per head of population. What this means is simply that humanity must rise above the stage at which its history is merely a process of natural history — this was how Marx always put it. The process of our species as a whole is still not consciously governed. History still does not progress at the level of human dignity, but more like a process of natural history, far too biological a process when taken as a whole. This is the problem we must consciously tackle, and we socialists first of all. Today it is a more pressing problem than the internal class struggle. This must be understood. I say that we shall not escape this bad situation unless we are ready, as Isaiah demanded of his people, to turn around, starting here in our own countries, the richest in the world but rich in a way that has become false. Here and nowhere else is the fly-wheel in motion that is driving the entire chariot of human existence towards the abyss, as it has been for the last 200 years, and now with a fearfully accelerating tempo. We are pulling everyone else with us, in the Second World of the Eastern bloc, in the oil-rich Third World and the starving Fourth World. We are pulling them all along our own road. And this is why it is we here who must change our life first of all.

In previous times, those who 'changed the world' often came from outside. Today there is no longer any outside. The problem is a global one, and we have to transform our civilisation constructively from within.

This means correctly recognising the contradictions 'internal' to the world as a whole, recognising them justly, in precisely the biblical sense. For instance, hatred is deliberately whipped up towards the OPEC countries, focussing at present on the situation in Iran. We must understand that the original causes of conflicts such as that taking place in Iran lie with us here. Not in a single country, but in the way our civilisation functions and has external effects that have destroyed the traditional structures elsewhere. The First World War and the Versailles treaty did less damage to Germany, less to shake up the life of our people, than the intervention of this Western lifestyle of ours with its often devastating by-products into these traditional milieus. In Europe the response to the post-war situation of 1918 was the most atrocious outbreak of barbarism of 1933-45 — fostered and promoted, used and installed by our ruling circles. And now Iran is being judged on the lines of the person who notices the speck in someone else's eye, but not the plank in his own.

The tragedy in Kampuchea is also our affair. Since atomic weapons have come into existence the old basic attitude of antagonism in social contradictions of all kinds, external and internal, has been put in question. Since the invention of atomic weapons! And these are only the tip of the iceberg of problems that industrial, technical and scientific development under capitalism has presented us with. Now that atomic weapons have come into being, we are faced with the necessity of treating social contradictions, both external and internal, in a new way. This was something that Khrushchev and Kennedy, for example, already recognised. Khrushchev, indeed, whom many left sectarians so dreadfully disparage, since they fail to understand the significance his appearance had for both internal and external Soviet policy, under the concrete conditions of the Soviet Union. It is very easy to know everything better from outside. I believe we must eliminate the Old Testament eye-for-eye, tooth-for-tooth principle from our approach to the social question, to the internal class struggle. To seek salvation in bringing contradictions to a head is no longer any good 'internally' either, now that it is no good 'externally', i.e. because externally the East-West contradiction prevails, and still more so the North-South contradiction. The manner in which internal class contradictions function and are waged here is inseparable from this new world situation. Contradictions must still be resolved. But the mode and the rules of this resolution must be considered afresh. In future, adversaries in both foreign and domestic policy must also be seen as allies. It is necessary to engage with them not less but more, to struggle still more with them. But this means doing more than just exchanging statements; it means engaging in dialogue, in genuine ideological debate. And this debate means sitting down together at a table; for it is necessary to contend with everyone to arrive at a new formulation of the problems of our society. Anyone we refuse to discuss with will quite unavoidably stand against us. And they will do so in a way, and also in forms of struggle, in which they might well not stand against us if we would engage in dialogue with them. We must raise all questions of domestic and foreign policy in the perspective of survival, for example no longer aiming at the unconditional victory of our own class, our own country, our own system. What nonsense, for example, at a time like this to still try and change frontiers, to put right the results of past wars. The ecology crisis is not only the comparatively minor problem of limited resources and destruction of the environment which is the first thing that strikes us; we must also recognise the comprehensive mechanisms which drive this crisis along.

Some Preconditions for Resolving the Ecology Crisis

In order to keep in mind the whole field of challenges a Green movement faces, and which it must tackle in concrete political terms, I want to indicate some conditions that may serve to characterise the comprehensive framework of ecological politics:

— The ecology crisis is insoluble unless we work at the same time at overcoming the confrontation of military blocs. It is insoluble without a resolute policy of détente and disarmament, one that renounces all demands for subverting other countries. Growth will continue as long as the arms race continues. We must be clear about that. And the next and most ominous step in the arms race would be the installation of new missiles in this country.

Anyone who wants first of all to 'liberate' any other countries and peoples, and especially to 'redeem' a country so close at hand as the GDR, has understood too little, far too little, about the present situation. The GDR is a rich country, if not quite as rich as West Germany.

— The ecology crisis is insoluble without a new world economic order on the North-South axis. And we must realise that our entire standard of living is largely based on the exploitation and suppression of the rest of humanity. Anyone who views abandoning this standard of living and sharing resources simply as a loss, or alternatively simply as a capitalist solution, still has a great deal to relearn.

— The ecology crisis is insoluble without a decisive breakthrough towards social justice in our own country and without a swift equalisation of social differences throughout Western Europe. This equalisation requires a united Western Europe. A Europe that is not a Europe of the monopolies, but is concerned above all that the peoples of Southern Italy, of Portugal and Greece are brought to something like the level of the developed countries, which alone will open the more comprehensive possibility of solidarity with the Third and Fourth Worlds. For injustice at home prevents us from being just on the world scale. It ties people's energies here to the competition to have as much as someone else who's got a bit more, and this on the whole scale of minor differences, so that it is simply impossible to raise the major problem, the North-South problem.

— The ecology crisis is insoluble without progress in human emancipation here and now, even while capitalism still exists. It is insoluble without countless individuals managing to rise above their immediate and compensatory interests. The freedom of the individual is now becoming the condition for survival, a freedom which includes the possibility of raising oneself above this orientation to mere immediate interests, given that this is necessary for life. Thoreau said in the 19th century that every superfluous possession was a restriction on freedom. This points to the need for a psychological revolution, i.e. the creation of its social and ideological preconditions. I have already quoted elsewhere the biblical injunction not to store up treasures on earth. The reason given for this is also worth quoting: 'For where your treasure is, there will your heart be also'. This is the problem of compensatory interests in the Christian formulation of the New Testament. It is worth reading on in this text, because its concern is to view in a positive sense the abandonment and renunciation of things that in the final analysis may well be superfluous, even a hindrance to full human development. In this sense I shall quote again from the text attributed to Christ, as an indispensable addition and completion to the commandment against storing up treasure. It goes on: 'Set your mind on God's kingdom and his justice before everything else'. What I have in mind here is of course not the specifically religious content of this formula, but rather what Christ has to say as a moral teacher of highest authority, whether we believe in him in the religious sense or not. What he has to tell us about the need to raise ourselves to a higher form of life more worthy of human beings, the need for self-realisation and self-transcendence towards other people and towards humanity and the whole of creation — indeed in any direction, so long as it remains within humanity and does not damage or destroy any other life. It is in this direction that we stand to profit if we abandon this storing up treasure.

— If all this is brought to a common denominator, the conclusion is as follows: The ecology crisis is insoluble under capitalism. We have to get rid of the capitalist manner of regulating our economy, and above all of this capitalist driving mechanism, for a start at least bringing it under control. In other words, there is no solution to the ecology crisis without the combination of all anti-capitalist and socialist tendencies for a peaceful democratic revolution against the dominant economic structure. A majority of this kind must come together democratically and pluralistically, if it is to have sufficient political power to extricate the state and administrative functions from control at all levels — local, provincial, national, continental and global — by all kinds of monopoly, private and special interests. These functions must rather be transformed into instruments of control over these special interests which restrict and endanger the lives and the conditions of development of the majority, and prevent us from raising the task of solidarity both in our own country and on a world scale. Freedom must be the freedom of the individual, not as is sometimes opposed to this the freedom of that peculiar 'collective subject' we call the monopolies, and similar super-institutions. Would the freedom of the individual human being stand and fall with these? That really can't be taken seriously, it is a very superseded point of view. These monopolies and super-institutions have scarcely anything in common with human enterprise in the broadest sense; except to be its most extreme perversion, carrying to absurdity the whole principle of human initiative which we must unconditionally maintain in our culture and civilisation.

The subject of my talk today was the socialist alternative and ecological politics, i.e. the linkage of these two concepts, which turn out to be one and the same when seen from the socialist side, inseparable in view of the coupling provided by the anti-capitalist orientation. From both the inner necessity of our goals and the external necessity of the danger of catastrophe we see impending, we strive for a historic compromise in good time on the broadest possible basis, i.e. a compromise between all forces that seek the preservation and further development of our own civilisation and world civilisation as a whole. In this country, the Green movement could be the embodiment of a great and necessary historic compromise of such kind. To be more precise, it could become so. In this sense, therefore, give the Green movement your strength!

Speech in Freiburg, November 1979

Towards a General Theory of the Historic Compromise

The point of departure is a positive and — given my particular theoretical and political purpose — a deliberately idealising adoption of the strategy of the 'historic compromise' developed by the Italian Communist Party. This formula was drafted pragmatically, and was applied at least partly in an opportunistic form. Its content is indeed reformist, yet in such a way that, if elaborated consistently, it can point towards an ideological mass mobilisation for *reforms with a revolutionary content*, for *reforms of a major and system-transcending kind*.

Contrary to how it may often seem, the 'historic compromise' presents the most active, most offensive and most realisable idea of transforming 'Western' bourgeois society since the Russian revolution. On the basis of this idea, I worked when I was in prison on the subject 'Background and Perspectives of the Historic Compromise'. I am convinced that this approach, which initially constitutes 'only' the turning-point and pivot of the Eurocommunist orientation, offers the *possibility of a more general theory* which leads far beyond the specific Italian conjuncture and the practice of the Italian Communist Party, indeed beyond the context of Eurocommunism in general.

For the first time since the Erfurt Programme of the German Social-Democrats, on which an approximate consensus of all socialists formed at the end of the 19th century, this formula again offers the prospect of a programmatic convergence of means and end in the world-wide movement for socialism. It needs a theoretical push in order to make use of this opportunity. A general theory of the historic compromise could become the ideological basis for a process of convergence, growing unity of action and ultimate reunification of all socialist tendencies in the highly industrialised and even the partially industrialised states (North America, Western Europe, Japan, Australia, important countries in Latin America, as well as some countries in other regions). The first requirement for such a theory is an acknowledgement of the far-reaching changes that have taken place since the end of the 19th century within bourgeois society and also outside of it — as a counter-movement to its global colonial expansion. Equally necessary is study of the concrete social and political situation in each geographic economic zone, only a small part of which of course can be carried out immediately. In this connection, the basic approach would be along the following lines:

According to Marx, the intensification of antagonistic class contradictions in the most developed capitalist countries was to lead there to a decisive social revolution, in the wake of which the problems of the less developed and colonialised peoples would find their solution by way of international solidarity and aid.

Now the polarisation of bourgeois society analysed in *Capital* has at least not been converted into the relation of psychological and political forces which was rationalistically expected. It is no longer probable that the crisis of bourgeois society will find its solution in the sense of the proletarian revolution traditionally expected.

A striking fact of the present situation seems rather to be the unambiguous *dominance of the external contradictions of bourgeois society over its internal contradictions*. The East-West and especially the North-South contradictions prevail. The internal class struggle over real wages, over working and living conditions, shows the tendency to become a subordinate function of bourgeois society in its confrontation with the Second, Third and Fourth Worlds, and it is here that both national and international destiny will be determined, far more than by the play of internal conflicts.

In conditions such as these, it would be anachronistic and dangerous to continue striving for solutions via an intensification of the internal class contradictions. The question is rather to bring these into relative adjustment, in such a way that at the same time an external adjustment becomes possible in the form of a radically changed world economic order.

I would emphasise most strongly the need for a comprehensive and convergent new orientation of all socialist forces in view of the ecological crisis that directly arises from the capitalist mode of production.

It is enough to give normal free rein to the prevailing and still globally dominant tendency of limitless expansion in the consumption of raw materials and energy, as well as the disturbance of the balance of nature by the most diverse consequences of our technology. In the course of a few decades the whole of human civilisation will then perish, and the very existence of the human species will be put in question and conjure up the most seriously antagonistic conflicts. This is a perspective of actual catastrophe that Marxism has generally failed to envisage. It will be impossible to prevent it without a *policy of historic compromise on the broadest basis, and in good time,* i.e. a policy of compromise between all forces concerned for the preservation and qualitatively higher development of our own civilisation and world civilisation in general.

To sum up, we find the conditions for the general emancipation of humanity that was and remains the unrelinquishable goal of the socialist movement to be fundamentally altered, in such a way as to require a consistent and coherent revision of our entire theoretical basis. Modern revolutionary theory will have to relate to classical Marxism in a similar way to the relationship of relativistic to classical physics.

Outline for a Research Project at Bremen University
Winter 1979

Why We Need to Re-examine Our Entire Theoretical Inheritance

(...) Many of you do not sufficiently realise what a colossal change is needed in our thinking, as far as the role of the working class is concerned. I am going to give you an analogy, so that you can better appreciate the angle from which I have now come to assess this. Just imagine — as a kind of experiment — that a Marxist-Leninist thinker had appeared two thousand years ago in Rome. And he had studied the class struggles of the 150 years since the Gracchi. The class struggles in Rome at the precise time of which Marx said that Roman history could be deciphered by the contradictions around the agrarian question or the peasant question, to put it in a much modernised form. The Gracchi were themselves a fraction of the dominant class. They led forward what was to become the popular party that later brought Caesar to power. In other words they had a populist orientation, an orientation to the masses 'from above'. But behind them stood a real mass movement, a movement of those peasants who were still free, or a movement of soldiers. The two things were virtually one and the same, as colonisation was already under way. And subsequently, even before the birth of Jesus, before Caesar still, there was the experience of the Spartacus insurrection. So our Marxist-Leninist ideologist could have established the tremendous role that internal class struggles played, and conclude from this that if the revolution of peasants and slaves could be led to victory in Rome, this would resolve the problems of the whole of the rest of the world — the Mediterranean world of the time. And what I am saying to you is that Marx in the 19th century had a quite analogous idea of the further course of world history, only with a different class subject, i.e. the proletariat. He seriously imagined that a proletarian revolution in England would liberate India. Can we really cling to a model that quite logically led to this conclusion, a conclusion since overtaken by events?

If you look at how things actually did proceed in Rome, you find that the internal class struggles, as far back as the time of the Gracchi (their revolts were from around 133 to 121 B.C.), were first of all influenced, far more than they seem if only the internal contradictions are examined, by external contradictions, i.e. by the Romans' colonial role. The struggles of the Gracchi would not have arisen without the Punic wars and the expansion of Rome that these brought about. Secondly, the function of these internal class struggles, in the last instance, was to transform the social situation at home in such a way that Rome was in a position to play its comprehensive colonial role in the Mediterranean region. It thus came about, to a far-reaching extent, that the needs of the subordinate class in Rome, even the needs of the domestic slaves — needs mediated of course by the power relations as a whole — meant that Roman legions had to be sent abroad. The famous formula 'bread and circuses' had a colonialist implication: cereals, gladiators, animals and whatever else had to be obtained so as to keep the parasitic metropolis quiet.

To sum all this up, the resulting situation in Roman history was in any case one in which the *external* contradictions were dominant. But these were not class contradictions in the strict sense. It is quite false for Marxism-Leninism to preach that in the present day, too, the confrontation of blocs is really just a protusion of internal class contradictions. Formerly we had proletariat and bourgeoisie in the same country, and now we have proletarian and bourgeois states at the world level. That is not the ways things are. In actual fact, external social contradictions in the Mediterranean world of the time proved to dominate over the internal contractions in Rome, in Italy, and these internal class contradictions led ultimately to colonialism. I would say that something similar is true today.

If you look at the present situation, you find at the purely empirical level a general process of integration of the working class into the system. You can of course discuss till the cows come home the presence of contrary tendencies, and from time to time there are moments when things look different. But in the long run and on the mass scale integration is the dominant tendency. However people may seek to excuse or explain this fact, it is undeniable that the struggle with the privileged classes at home for division of the product, a struggle which is quite justified when viewed in the local context, is precisely waged on the backs of the rest of humanity. In ancient Rome it was exactly the same. Each increase in real wages and thus in the average standard of living here only pulls the extreme ends of the scale of per capita income further apart, and this has such great effects that the sufferings of the underprivileged in our own country disappear by comparison. Here the question is rather one of suffering of a far more subjective kind, it is not a problem of material existence but a subjective, so-called *existential* problem, a problem of suppressed individuality. This takes place at a quite different level. Can we increase the causes of death and murder on the whole of the rest of the scale simply because we here need to have more in order to equalise with those above? You can of course say that this only happens because the popular forces have not prevailed in the European countries. But it could be that things go on in this way for another 20, 30 or 40 years. We cannot see any guarantee that the situation will change. And besides, given our traditional orientation, what are we to say to the masses 'the day after' if today we whisper in the ear of the bourgeoisie: 'Another bit better! Another bit more!' The same game could continue with our own finger on the trigger.

So far in history the subordinate classes have essentially always wanted, in the last instance, what the privileged classes already possessed. Their habits are governed by what is in the shop windows which they press their noses against. And when we consider the burdens inflicted on the planet by just a tenth of its human population with a standard of living on average that of West Germany, and how this would have to be multiplied by ten or twenty if everyone were to receive the same, then we can see that we simply no longer have the right to appeal without further examination to the needs of the masses as they presently are. I have already said that it is quite irresponsible to retreat to the position that history takes a long time to advance, that we have to be patient, to wait another 20 or 30 years in a state of illusion for the proletarian revolution to function in the way that Marx conceived of it in 1844 and subsequently.

In my opinion we have to undertake a revision of our entire socio-economic theory — though one on the basis of historical materialism. Dogmatic adherence to Marx is diametrically opposed to Marx's own historical materialism. It is directed against the perception of reality as it is.

We have to deploy the real achievement of Marxism, and relate to the rest of Marxism by seeing Marx from today's standpoint in a similar role to Newton. This means seeing that his theory (as opposed to his method, which we must continue to develop) had too specific a realm of validity, tied to a certain concrete historical situation. This theory was the special application of historical materialism to the analysis of competitive capitalism. Many laws that functioned at that time still function today. From a dogmatic standpoint, for example, it is marvellous to prove that exploitation today is greater than ever. Sure, in a mathematical sense! And yet this is no longer the lever that can overturn present conditions. All this love of figures, adding up hours spent on strike, numbers of strikers, etc. amounts to nothing at all.

We must ask ourselves, among other things, what the 'proletariat' really is in today's conditions, whose interests we should take up, and at the same time we have to realise that this *antagonistic* model for the solution of the contradiction between proletariat and bourgeoisie, which Marx put forward, cannot be transferred to the present situation, to the North-South constellation and to the East-West relationship, or else we shall all perish together. This means that what could still be achieved in Paris in 1871 by the internal class struggle, with barricades and cannons, no longer offers any human perspective at all in the conditions of today. We assumed that in one or other of the developed countries, and best in all of them at once, it was possible to strike a blow in the class struggle that would be fruitful for the whole of humanity. As long as this assumption seemed plausible, it was possible, if already problematic, to make a Jesuitic calculation — 'such and such a number of dead to avoid so and so many other deaths'. Today such a calculation is simply impossible. And all of this taken together, this total change in the overall situation, requires of us a readiness to re-examine our whole theoretical inheritance in a 'relativistic' sense, as I like to put it, suggesting that we should relate to Marx as Einstein related to Newton.

Excerpt from an interview for the Bunte-Liste-Zeitung, *December 1979*

The Truth About Anti-Communism

If we are to act correctly, indeed if we are to master the situation at all, we must I believe understand somewhat better why anti-communism is so deeply rooted. In the Federal Republic anti-communism is particularly deep. I need not mention the particular reasons for this in our national history. But the following remarks may be useful.

In Germany and in Europe in general there was first of all an anti-communism that reacted to the *Communist Manifesto*. This first anti-communism did not however succeed in frightening large sections of the working population themselves.

Then there was an anti-communism that no longer reacted simply to the *Communist Manifesto* as a piece of paper and a narrow movement this inspired, but rather to the Paris Commune of 1871 and to a powerful workers' movement. This second anti-communism had still less success in terrifying the broad working masses; it did not even prevent large sections of the bourgeois intelligentsia, the petty-bourgeois intelligentsia in particular, from flocking into the Social-Democrat party in Germany at the end of the last century, when this still had an unblemished Marxist programme. Why has anti-communism obtained such tremendous virulence since 1917, and even more so since 1945? Something new must have taken place. And here I have to refer to the ideas developed in *The Alternative*. What is it then that people react to when they hear we are communists?

Since 1917 — and in Germany particularly since 1945, when the other system confronted us in our own country — the bourgeois societies of the West, and we must admit that this includes the working masses, see themselves faced with a socialism (as the Eastern system calls itself) or a communism (as it is called here) *established on the basis of a civilisation different from that of Western Europe*. And this 'communism' — not that anyone pays any attention to our quotation marks — contains, whether deliberately so or not, the indirect threat of overthrowing the *entire* way of life here, i.e. including those habits that every man and woman has grown accustomed to. This overthrow not only threatens to affect certain relations of political power, but to bring about a cultural change whose model and mode of appearance in Russia the masses here absolutely cannot want. This has nothing to do with a critique of the Russian revolution seeking to destroy the system that has ensued. Such criticism can only originate over there. It simply means that in the name of socialism — or of communism as it is described from outside — a completely different social order has come into being than that which we promised ourselves under the names of socialism and communism as a progressive continuation of West European civilisation. And this constellation has the unavoidable result that anti-communism today is not a reaction to the socialism and communism of Marx, but rather to that social structure and political system which has arisen in the Soviet Union. Whether this makes us angry or not — and no matter how unjust it may be to us — the suspicion attached to our name is a reality. It means that people reject any challenge that seeks to bring this kind of socialism or communism into existence in this country, and they do so spontaneously and with psychological necessity, with a mass-psychological necessity. What this means for us socialists and communists in Western Europe is the demand, the very pressing demand, that we should present ourselves and our theory in such a way that this impression is never given. Do we really act in the way this requires?

Excerpt from an interview for the Bunte-Liste-Zeitung, *December 1979*

From Prague to Kabul

I thought at the time, and subsequently wrote, that the military action against the Prague reform movement was the greatest crime of the Soviet leaders since the Second World War![2] This is no longer quite correct. If we had managed to achieve something at that time in Prague, and subsequently in Warsaw, even in Berlin 'capital of the GDR', and if Moscow had accordingly shown even a trace of adaptation to a new reality of this kind on its West European periphery, then there would not have been the invasion of Afghanistan today. Whatever the council of elders in the Kremlin may have had in mind, this is a crime against peace that extends far beyond Afghanistan, far beyond the Kabul meridian. It is a crime against détente and disarmament. It puts in the shade the subjugation of the Prague spring. It even goes beyond Deng Xiao-ping's unashamed 'lesson' to Vietnam.

Back in 1968 the flagrant breach of international law had a defensive motivation which the whole of world public opinion could appreciate. In all countries of the Soviet bloc the Novotny's[13] were trembling for their positions of power, terrified to the marrow and to the Moscow centre. By flexing their military muscles right from the early months of 1968, they themselves brought about the mood in Czechoslovakia that might have eventually led to the country leaving the Warsaw Pact. Yet this was an established member of the 'socialist community'. Despite all differences, it shared the same basic social and political structure. In this case, the Soviet Union did have something to lose — against the background of its sacrifice in liberating Czechoslovakia in the struggle against Hitlerite Germany. So even though the 1968 intervention shattered a hope held by all democrats and socialists (and from no other standpoint is this so inexcusable as from our own), at least it did not directly endanger peace and survival.

All questions of the fate of humanity depend on peace, détente and disarmament. The intervention in Afghanistan now shows us that these values and goals do not take first place in Soviet aspirations, that they are ready to use means that fly directly in the face of these values and goals. This action cannot have any other result but to fuel the arms-race psychology throughout the world. It is helping to drive on the ominous process by which in a relatively very short space of time the basic conditions of life for the human species on this earth are being destroyed.

Afghanistan may become the Vietnam adventure of a Soviet leadership that is showing as never before the naked face of great-power chauvinism, of bureaucratic imperialism. What is particularly worthy of consideration is that these leaders, isolated from their own people, live so little in the world as it actually is that they are honestly frightened by their own reflection. They are quite serious about feeling misunderstood. I would believe it if someone told me one of them was actually in tears. Everything is designed to destroy the remaining trust bound up with the non-capitalist basis of the Soviet Union, its objective task of aiding the rise of the underdeveloped countries.

In summer 1968 we hoped they wouldn't dare, but we didn't see the invasion as unlikely — for the reasons I've mentioned. In Afghanistan we certainly had to see an invasion as possible, but we didn't need to see it as likely. We were taught a bitter lesson. It is as if the Moscow Politburo wanted to prove the Chinese and Franz-Josef Strauss correct in their view of them. These men in the Kremlin, all far too old, *must* have known that their action would destroy the atmosphere for détente and arms limitation, that they were handing the arms lobby on the other side weighty arguments for a new round of the arms race that was in any case being planned. They *must* have known they were giving the other side's plans to intervene for the 'security of oil supplies' the seal of approval, plans that again were already on the table. But it is clear that they no longer count even marginally on the psychological factor of a public opinion that is gradually yet unambiguously making progress, on the resistance of countless people on this side of the bloc frontier to the uninhibited play of power interests. Their only dialogue is with the Pentagon. They are bringing about a situation in which the Third World countries have to use one hand to defend themselves against Moscow instead of both against Washington and NATO. With this invasion they are functioning entirely as accomplices of world reaction. They are taking on a role we have never wanted them to play: as one of the two superpowers who wage their deadly rivalry on the backs of the peoples.

How has the tragedy of the Afghan people come about? For over twenty years the Soviet Union had been building up its positions there in a combination of (objectively) anti-imperialist solidarity and conventional power politics. The internal contradictions of this very backward country were profound enough to bring into being an autonomous national-revolutionary resistance movement, which given local conditions could only have its nucleus and its leadership in the intelligentsia (including the military). The big neighbour, however, intervened to guide and deform this — at least indirectly, if not directly. This constellation suggested to the Afghan avant-garde both their model and their mistaken timescale. In 1978 it was not a revolution that Nur Mohammed Taraki and his comrades made, but rather a putsch, so as to bestow the approved revolution on their people from above. With good intentions, I believe, they decreed an agrarian reform that broke up the framework of peasant life in such a way that the peasants did not gain anything with the land they were given. Effectively, the Afghan peasants met the same fate as the Iranian peasants under the Shah. What was planned as a benefit struck the whole country and people as an unforseeable misfortune.

The Afghan excursion was already lost in advance, given the simultaneous revolution in Iran; this gives an unbeatable support to the Islamic resistance, which of course is bound up with the traditional forces. The Soviet invaders will not lose Afghanistan to the Americans, but to the Moslems. And we can only wish this lesson on them. As against the Prague spring, this time they have committed a serious mistake even from the standpoint of the most orthodox interests of the apparatus. Kabul can therefore have more direct effects on domestic Soviet policy. It is still too early to say where the lunacy of pouring oil onto the Islamic fire may lead. Kabul underlines how necessary it is for the peoples of the Soviet Union and its allies to pension off their Novotny's and fundamentally transform their whole political superstructure. And left organisations in the West must quickly unburden themselves of representatives who provide cover for the Soviet leaders even in their Afghan adventure. Anyone who welcomes this intervention simply shows that they are formed in the same mould as the ruling bureaucratic apparatus.

I am of the opinion, moreover, that the forces of reason here in the West now face a great responsibility: in no way to support the escalation of tension pursued by ruling circles both in the USA and the Soviet Union, and — in West Germany in particular — to defend the Ostpolitik that was pursued by the socialist-liberal coalition in its best days. Peace, détente, and disarmament — right now!

December 1979

Why, as a Socialist,
I'm Joining the Green Party

Dear friends and comrades,

It is precisely because of the extremely broad spectrum it is bringing together at its foundation that the Green party is going to be an important experiment worth the most careful attention, and not just in West Germany. Only in this way does it offer the chance of establishing in the long run a fruitful new constellation of forces in opposition to the ossified pattern of existing party politics. Political forces in this country are 'wrongly arranged'. A new grouping has arrived on the scene, a grouping formed on new criteria rather than a new division within the old model. Is the Green party going to make a contribution to this? How clear are we about the extraordinariness of this attempt?

I intend to 'translate into Swedish' in order to make clear what we are trying to do — without claiming that the comparison is completely exact. In Sweden there are two parties with a resolutely ecological orientation. One of them is the conservative Centre party, which at present holds the premiership, a party that comes originally from the country and was a peasants' party. The other is the Left (Communist) party, a party that is no longer Stalinist but has set its sights in a new direction, and has its second base of mass support — besides the ecology problem — in the women's movement. The Greens are the attempt to bring together under one roof the forces that in other countries form at least two parties in the traditional constellation, because they are indeed very different as regards their origins. The wing of the movement coming from the left expressly welcomes this attempt, even if not all its representatives are yet clear as to the consequences this option has for their actions. I hope that the majority of those Greens who do not come from the left welcome it too. The points are clearly in the process of a long-term shift. We should all be aware of this. It would be unwise to quarrel at this stage in the proceedings.

If I have not taken a stand in favour of an organisationally separate socialist alternative, it is because I believe that a Green party which practises within itself the historic compromise that is needed would in West German conditions be the best long-run solution, and something really new. We socialists intend to press our claims openly, in the spirit of a dialogue in which each partner seriously seeks to understand the other. But considerations of principle will not lead us to pursue the fruitless and illusory course of painting the green cause red. The Greens are not a left or socialist auxiliary.

Our reasons can be explained very simply. Without overcoming the ecology crisis, which puts in question the very existence of human civilisation on this earth, the mere possibility of the socialist goal — the general emancipation of human beings, men and women — becomes an illusion. If there are those among the socialists planning to enter the Green party who still talk in terms of camouflage, so that they can present a clean image to comrades who raise the class question, they have still not understood the problem completely. Marx and Engels specifically recognised the possibility of a historical situation leading to the common ruin of the contending classes, i.e. at a time when a civilisation is perishing and there is no revolutionary class able to make a new start. In my view, the traditional class struggle between wage-labour and capital, as it is now customarily managed by employers' associations and trade unions, shows all the signs of a stalemate.

Some comrades, whose way of thinking is fixated on a past era that cannot be brought back, speak staunchly of a 'still (too) low level of class struggle'. You still fail to see that the emperor has no clothes. The world-historic mission of the proletariat was an illusion, in so far as this idea assumes the working class as it actually is, and was even at its best times. It was precisely here that Marx was wrong. Do you really think that by clinging to the little finger of short-run and immediate working-class interests you can eventually get the whole hand: socialism via a Spartacist insurrection,[14] via proletarian revolution? Very many workers, as human beings, will advance with us beyond the vicious circle of a distribution struggle that simply perpetuates the relation of wage-labour and capital. We must think of quite new combinations if we are looking for the mass social force for a solution to the crisis at the general social level, and the form in which this is to be found.

Today socialists are not needed in order to be more trade-unionist than the trade unions. On the one hand, the DGB [German Trade-Union Federation] does this already, by and large, and we are far from denying the relative importance of wage struggles. On the other hand, we can never get to the roots of existing conditions through the DGB and SPD as they are. The struggle to overcome the ecology crisis takes precedence over a class struggle of this kind, which has no perspective of superseding the present system — indeed, which takes place in such a way that each new turn of the roundabout of rationalisation, inflation and wage bargaining simply fuels the boiler for an explosion that is unavoidable if it continues. The struggle for a just distribution within the rich countries need not be abandoned, but it must be given a new context. This does not mean giving ourselves a green camouflage simply because the prospects for anything else are not good — it means being green. I am radically ecological in my views. Each per cent increase in production is too much, since each per cent additional consumption of finite and irreplaceable natural resources is an injury to the rest of humanity, as well as to our own children and grandchildren. And you can no longer say 'Father forgive them, for they know not what they do'. All those who call the Greens a single-issue movement fail to see the wood for the trees. What the Greens are proposing affects everything. To take only the following points:

— The ecology crisis is insoluble without overcoming the confrontation between the Eastern and Western blocs, which drives on the arms race and economic growth on both sides, and is thus doubly suicidal.

— The ecology crisis is insoluble without a new world economic order on the North-South axis. We can see how in response to our exploitative and culture-destroying encroachments a second bloc confrontation is arising and threatens to be at least as murderous as the first, if in other forms.

— The ecology crisis is insoluble without social justice in the industrially developed countries. And this cannot mean anything but an adjustment in favour of those who have a bad deal in what is still a capitalist society. After all, it isn't the workers who drive the motor of this economic lunacy. Only if we are clear about this do we have a prospect of opposing the restraint policies pursued by the monopolies and the power apparatus with a restraint policy of our own, a policy in the interest of the great majority, as is so evidently needed.

— Because of this, moreover, the ecology crisis is insoluble without the advance of human emancipation, without rising here and now above the compensatory needs for consumption, prestige and power, so that despite the conditions still prevailing we need to seek a new, alternative way of life for all.

— In conclusion, the ecology crisis is insoluble — and this follows from everything above — without a movement of *conversion* that brings together the most diverse alternative attempts in thinking and living, a movement that attains a degree of cohesion and agreement such as was reached in the past only through the claims of religion. Today, however, more rationality must be brought into play if we are to go beyond the present economic order. The ecology crisis will force the end of capitalism. But we must contribute more towards this than abstract ideas of expropriation.

Anyone who today wants to be a Marxist in the theoretical sense must take on one task above all others: to circumscribe ecologically the traditional political economy of both capitalism and socialism, and consider afresh how social appropriation is possible — given that expropriation has sometimes succeeded alright in the past, but social appropriation never. Once this is done, nothing in our economic theory will look the same as it did before — with two exceptions: the goal of general emancipation and the starting-point of the analysis. This continues to be capitalism, the capitalist economic order of this society. The present ecological crisis has been conjured up by a 200-year course of capitalism. All other systems, the Eastern system above all, have been drawn into this dance by capitalism, and are establishing the same relationship with nature in a struggle of enforced competition. Of course, the dilemma in the other bloc has long since acquired a dynamic of its own. What should be clear from all this is that we are not against the traditional workers' movement. It is just that this is no longer enough (. . .)

The destiny of a Green party at this point in time will depend decisively on the level of its internal communication and tolerance. In order to move 'ahead' it must succeed in bringing together elements from heterogenous origins. This is possible because these have a common denominator in their ecological and thus objectively anti-capitalist orientation. 'Neither right, nor left, but ahead' can be a good way of conceiving ourselves, so long as we are completely clear that right and left are still a reality within the Green movement, and will remain so for a long time to come. It would be mistaken to assume that red and green confront one another. For there are reds or leftists who have understood the priority of the ecological challenge and thus become at the same time genuine Greens. And there are people from all other lines of the political spectrum through to quite far on the right who have equally understood the priority of the ecological challenge. Green is the third element, the connecting link.

The social necessity of a Green alternative seems readily apparent to me. I am quite convinced that in the long run it can break through. Whether it is doing so already depends on how far those involved have themselves understood the ecology crisis. If you seriously believe that the question is one of survival, and survival in a timescale that is within our own horizon, how can you start proposing expulsions? Proscriptions of this kind are only needed for organisations who compete against one another in elections. And there they are superfluous, since everyone understands them. They may be superfluous against other groupings, if the Green party experiment succeeds. My personal belief is that it would mean an advance for our left positions (and not only in connection with the Green party) if the groups with a centralist structure were to dissolve themselves![5]But if the members of these groups take an honest part in the work of the Green party, we have to give them time for the process of discussion and education that is needed.

It would be naive in terms of organisational policy to prohibit special interest groups in the context of a party with several wings. On the other hand, no one should exclude themselves. If anyone can join, comrades, then why don't you? Otherwise you've only yourselves to blame if it turns out disappointing. I hereby announce my own adherence to the Green party. I am not joining in order to play the role of chief ideologist, but to be a committed ordinary member. And when, as in *Stern* magazine, seven men already declare themselves for the Greens, then besides them one must place seven women. In the traditional Chinese proverb, women hold up half the sky. An alternative party must also be committed to overcoming patriarchy.

With reference to the problems posed by the Federal elections and the situation in the 1980s, the left, socialist wing — both inside and outside the Greens, inside and outside the SPD — needs a new form of collaboration beyond the former fragmented groups, without meaning a conventional and closed party organisation. We must organise our self-conception and our theoretical work more effectively and more cooperatively. In this sense I am in favour of a general 'Socialist Conference' to be held this spring [1980].

The section of the Green movement coming from the left needs to catch up as regards its ideological mastery of the ecological crisis. We must for example first read the celebrated book by Herbert Gruhl before we pass judgement on certain slogans that don't suit us. For myself, I know of no more important document as regards our role in a Green dialogue, in the sense of the challenge that needs to be positively taken up. The question is whether we want to enter into a genuine discussion or not. In this book problems are brought to light for which we Marxists and socialists have no adequate answer from our own tradition. My own former view of things is also inadequate.

If we react ideologically and mentally in different ways to certain facts (and these are facts we are only just coming to grips with), that is no reason to disqualify the other position in a way that rules out any dialogue, or — what would be far worse — to close one's eyes to the facts themselves. I find it quite atrocious that there are Marxists who contest the finite scope of the earth's exploitable crust. I think something is seriously wanting if people can read Gruhl's book without being struck by the seriousness, both objective and subjective, of what it contains. Unfortunately there is still no book that we can recommend the section of the Green movement who come from the right — or more broadly the section that is not Marxist or socialist — to read with the same urgency. As far as the Green movement is concerned we have a major work ahead of us, corresponding to a major share of responsibility.

The tension that arises from heterogeneity of origin can only be handled productively if it is not denied, if people do not try simply to overlook it. People must not deny where they have come from, and no one, on any side, should be required to do so. At the start of a process of unification, its goal shouldn't be assumed to be already attained. That makes the process impossible. If lazy compromises are extracted or conceded in advance, that only lays the seeds of a more poisonous infection. If the differences of origin and the differences in the particular aspirations that flow into the Green cause were suppressed, this would simply lead in practice to always defining other people as 'right' or 'left', but oneself as always 'ahead'. The way ahead can only be found by dealing with these realities.

Within the Green movement, and in the far smaller space of a Green party, we should wage a struggle not against the right nor against the left, but for a convergence of ideas and — where there is nothing else — an avowed and principled compromise based on recognising the coexistence of different points of view. Of course, ideological differences cannot be set aside by majority decision. We must struggle to dissolve mutual misunderstandings and prejudices that divide people by ideology or by generation, if we are to find out what it is around us that is really intolerable and how important this is in view of new historical tasks. This requires active work at deepening and making more precise the perspective that we pursue in common.

Speech at the founding congress of the Green party in Karlsruhe,
January 1980

Goodbye to Capitalism – Goodbye to our Concept of the Proletariat

What those internal contradictions of capitalism to which the traditional concept of the proletariat is related have so far not managed to bring about *by themselves alone* will be brought about by the ecology crisis: the ecology crisis will force us to say goodbye to capitalism. For the very real danger of total catastrophe that we can see ahead is the quintessence of what we have been accustomed to call the general crisis of capitalism. It is inseparably connected with competition for maximum profit, which today is waged not by the relatively harmless manufacturers and joint-stock companies of the 19th century, but rather by national and international super-monopolies who play with the fate of whole states and peoples. The destruction of the natural basis of human existence altogether, and on a world scale, poses the old question of 'socialism or barbarism' with an intensity that earlier socialists, for all their far-sightedness, did not even dream of. Besides, we should not now dispute primarily about socialism, for in most cases this simply means disputing about models. Let us remember the famous phrase of Marx, that socialism — he says communism — is not a prefigured ideal which we want to put into practice, but rather the real movement that supersedes the existing state of things. The existing state of things, which we have to extricate ourselves from together with the people who are that state of things and collude in it, is precisely the capitalist one.

As far as the real movement is concerned, it seems to me that many comrades fail to see the wood for the trees, since they still adhere to an outdated concept. Some of them accuse me of a really grotesque mistake, i.e. of having forgotten the forces that lie in the factories and which the SPD and trade-union bureaucracy claims for itself. True, I have so far not expressed myself positively on this question; I have only emphasised, as required by the situation, what in my opinion is no longer valid. In any case, I would ask people to concede that to abandon a certain concept need not necessarily mean ceasing to pay attention to the objects (in this case therefore the subjects) that are subsumed by it, and to their interests.

A Theoretical Obstacle

The question stands as follows. The revolutionary subject is not 'functioning' in the way we were led to expect by our former concept of the proletariat and the whole context in which this was located. And we can look round in vain for a revolutionary working class, which is more or less like looking for radio sources with an optical telescope. The radio sources are there, and in our present case I assume that the sources of visible light are also among them. In the trade unions, for example, there are the Action Circles for Life. These still appear in the visible spectrum, but we should precisely avoid *reducing* them to the traditional workers' movement. They lie in another waveband, the band of radio sources, so to speak. Of course there is a continuity, just as there is in nature, and yet we now have to emphasise the aspect of a break in continuity, as far as the question of how we conceive of the revolutionary subject is concerned.

I believe we are faced here with a theoretical gap, which acts as an obstacle in our path. To summarise the problem once again as briefly as possible: is the overcoming of capitalism, the transition to socialism, really bound up with the concrete subject of the 'proletariat' that Marx indicated? Whatever we may meanwhile have added in the way of auxiliary hypotheses, and even considering that Marx himself, especially in the *Grundrisse*, viewed the question in a somewhat different way — in the prevailing interpretation this meant the European and North American proletariat of the 19th century, subordinated to a capitalism based on free competition. Given the very real material wretchedness it was capitalist exploitation *as such*, the contradiction between wage-labour and capital, that was *directly* supposed to provoke the revolt leading to socialism, since the workers had nothing to lose but their chains. We could analyse the reasons in more detail, but it seems evident to me that today exploitation provokes a reaction not directly as such, but rather by way of its various more remote consequences in the power that capital has at its disposal. The successes of the workers' movement in the distribution struggle were by the same token steps that led deeper into the overall system of bourgeois society. *If there is anything today that really does deserve the label of a single-issue movement, it is the institutionalised wage struggle which is ultimately subordinated completely to the overall process of capitalist reproduction.* This is indeed a front in the class struggle, but it is an old front. And if you locate the *centre of gravity there* and try to build up a perspective on this basis, you are objectively orientating yourselves to a backward front on which no breakthrough is possible.

Every Orthodoxy Eventually Becomes Reactionary

Comrades of the Fourth International have called my view pessimistic.[16]
Doesn't this rather reflect their own perspective? According to them, if
the traditional conception they defend won't work, then nothing will
work at all. Objectively, they play off the short-run interests of the
workers, which they adhere to unflinchingly and in a way devoid of
prospects, against long-run interests which quite overshadow the
achievements of any pragmatic opportunism. What a theoretical
blindness, seeing nothing outside the factory gates, to disparage the
upsurge of ecological awareness as a single-issue movement, while
participating in it now and then with an elitist critical distance that
defines their allies right from the start as having a limited point of view!
Every orthodoxy reaches the point where it becomes reactionary,
precisely when a new *epoch* in the liberation struggle is impending,
involving a fundamental regrouping of forces, and this orthodoxy then
tries to push people back into the patterns prescribed by the old
theoretical paradigm that must now be dialectically superseded. We
cannot wait until our old recipes start to work after all. But perhaps the
'socialist forces' are not identical with the forces that will press forward to
socialism in synchrony with the resolution of the ecological crisis? Not
identical in scale, first of all. Perhaps there are far more forces ready for
socialism than the socialist forces imagine? Perhaps a certain socialist
identity actually stands in the way of socialism? Very much will depend
on whether we socialists recognise the urgency of our task.

From the Dominance of Internal to the Dominance of External Contradictions

In all this we are still dealing simply with the narrow context of our
European situation. The idea of the world-historic mission of the
working class assumes that its class interests are *directly* identical not only
with those of its nation as a whole, but also with those of all humanity.
The workers are not just to liberate themselves into true human beings,
they are also to liberate all human beings. Marx promised in all
seriousness — and I am very far from making fun of him behind his back
— that a proletarian revolution in Europe and especially in England
would also free India. What happened was something very different than
Marx and those of us who followed him imagined, and not simply in the
East but here as well. The dynamic of internal class contradictions in the
most developed capitalist countries, which we traditionally saw as the
source of our general solution, has been overtaken by three external
contradictions. I shall simply indicate these in the historical sequence in

which they have piled up on one another.

First: East — West; second: North — South; third: humanity — nature.

'Humanity' is conceived here, of course, as the ensemble of social relations, but on a world scale, and particularly on the assumption that though non-capitalist relations of production are already to be found, the horizon of capitalist civilisation, i.e. the structure of productive forces moulded by capitalism, has nowhere yet been broken through. I assume the dominance of these external contradictions. Of course, from the standpoint of the totality — and this is the decisive point — these contradictions are external only with respect to the rich capitalist countries taken by themselves. Given this constellation, it is obvious that the workers in the rich countries, viewed as a class, have particular interests of their own.

The Fate of Humanity – Too Much for an Oppressed Class?

If proceeding from these assumptions we are seeking a hegemonic project and want to keep to the level of the overall interest of humanity — which is what Marx had in mind with the world-historic mission of the proletariat — we must go beyond Marx's own concept and direct ourselves to a more general subject than the Western working class of today. Like the utopian socialists and communists who Marx sought to dispense with, we must once again take the species interest as our fundamental point of reference — only now in a more concrete manner. It might well have been no more than a Hegelian error to have burdened a particular class, and a class restricted by its position in the reproduction process, with the fate of humanity as a whole.

We could also mention, moreover, that up till now there has not been a single case in world history where the typical subordinate class of a social formation has by itself anticipated the impending new order. Once again, the question is not where the individuals belonging to this class stand in the upheaval, whether the French peasants fight in the revolutionary army or in the Vendée. Neither the 'freedmen' or state slaves of the Asiatic mode of production, nor the Roman slaves, nor the peasants of the Middle Ages, made history in the epoch that followed. If the proletariat was supposed to act differently, this was a hypothesis whose confirmation seems to have become rather improbable in the light of historical experience. This certainly does not mean that the elements constituting the classes of the old society did not play their part in the revolutionary renovation. The most active elements from the former oppressed class were naturally one of the most important leavens in the new historic bloc. But this bloc is not simply an 'alliance', let alone a hotch-potch of elements from the various former classes and strata. It is only this in so far as its past aspect is examined, i.e. in a connection which is not fundamental as far as future perspective is concerned. This is why nothing pleases the orthodox sociologists, who are mentally tied to the decline of a certain order of things, so much as to demonstrate the heterogeneity of the forces involved. And as far as the elements that dominate at the start — i.e. in an uprising — are concerned, these sociologists fail to recognise the source of their mobilisation. This lies in the positive driving forces which are produced by the old order yet press beyond it, and not in the 'main contradiction' of the old order itself. What is liberated today — in the face of a challenge like no other before — is the 'surplus consciousness' produced by the general intellectualisation of labour with the advance of the capitalist productive forces. This is a result of the overall process of reproduction and its contradictions, and in its relatively most concentrated form it attacks outside the sphere of production proper. This can already be read in Marx's *Grundrisse*.

We have moreover seen the course of the 1968 reform movement in Czechoslovakia, on the basis of the same productive forces that are met with here in West Germany in a more developed form. On this point I would like to note that in 1969, after the Soviet intervention, the process also reached the factories. The idea of councils, the idea of self-management, took root among the production workers in the stricter sense. I see a regular law in this. Marx already saw the main content of the socialist phase as overcoming the opposition between mental and manual labour. And around this contradiction, the resolution of which has now become a central focus of history, forces line up in a new way. It is clear that the new historic bloc cannot in itself rise above this contradiction, in which it is itself formed. It will unavoidably bear this contradiction within it, in view of both its origin and its structure. The 'party' — to use this word for once in a very general sense — the party of liberty, equality and fraternity does not need to bemoan the unavoidable initial dominance of the intellectual elements. We must take note of it, and must be aware of the danger it involves — a danger which Marx already foresaw in his *Theses on Feuerbach*, about the 'educator and the educated' — and it must spur us to a readiness to overcome our special interests as intellectuals, time and time again. At least asymptotically, the process must reach its goal of general emancipation, the full and free development of all. In concrete terms, the process must grip the majority of people in their factories and offices. I would like to add that the 'intellectual elements' do not just enter this process as a social stratum of the old society, but that this concept includes all those who through their natural human endowment manage to reach an ability to reflect upon society, thanks to — and often despite — the conditions in which they have to struggle. I recall Gramsci's note that a worker who joins the party and studies its texts becomes an intellectual.

What is Meant by 'Working-Class Interests'?

Many comrades seem to falter when it comes to the question of the structure of needs of the masses who we represent. We know this is simply the reverse side of the capitalist market mechanism, but in practice we concede they are right if they want nothing more than a bit more and a bit better of what capitalism is already offering them. 'You deserve it, so long as capitalism is still continuing in its contradictions instead of perishing from them.' Even without the ecology crisis we would be faced with the need to organise on a mass scale an escape from the value orientations dictated by the market, since this is one of the most stubborn self-inhibiting mechanisms on the emancipatory forces. But now we know that our whole civilisation cannot continue with its centre of gravity in the present technology and the corresponding mass production. And this is true in a timespan that falls at least within the lifetime of our children or grandchildren. What do the 'interests of the working class' mean in such a situation? Must we not set ourselves the task of bringing demands such as that for job security (which in any case is now absolutely incompatible with the existing system, and no longer only relatively so) and demands for guaranteed real wages into our project in a new way, in fact relegating them to second place? The interests of working people today extend further than ever before beyond the sphere in which the distribution struggle is fought out, and in which these interests are right from the start deceived and recuperated. In the really lean years, when the approaching catastrophe becomes acute, even when the material wherewithal for our greedy production machine starts to be wanting, the traditionally underprivileged classes and strata of society will certainly be hardest hit. This will happen if we let the chariot roll on, while in our left ghetto we forge the cadres for our great day 'in the future'.

Apart from this, however, our strategy is not primarily one of renunciation in any sense. The question is to unchain and unleash our forces precisely where they are tied to the bourgeois way of life and help to reproduce it. The rise of the workers as human beings no longer depends on their being able to consume more, but rather on a new order for our entire life-process, on a transformation which is both political and cultural, reaching right into their subjectivity, their personal capacity as human beings. Even our concept of the worker ties us to bourgeois society, leading us to fixate the reduction of working human beings to workers, hence also defining their interests in the reduced form constrained by capitalism. I suspect that many orthodox Marxists do not trust the workers with this elevation as human beings, since they cannot have helped seeing for so long how the workers were unwilling to follow their calls to battle. Neo-mechanical materialism really is trapped in a vicious circle, i.e. that the capitalism which is the cause of proletarian subalternity would have to vanish in order to overcome this. No, even if the present upsurge is not beginning in the factories, because there capitalism holds sway over human beings most completely, consuming their energy in the most total way without their being able to reproduce themselves in human terms at their work — it will still not pass the factories by.

'It's Always Other People Who're Philistines'

We are generally agreed that some 80 to 85 per cent of our society belong to the wage-earning class in the broadest sense, and hence to a concept of the 'proletariat' that is modern at least in scope. But what sociology is it that labels the Greens a middle-class movement? Because they have 'too many teachers', I heard a Social-Democrat comrade say in Heidelberg. It was one of the good traditions of the old Social-Democrat party in Germany that it did not permit manual and mental work to be set against one another. In our present sociology, we should most decisively proceed from the concept of the collective worker as performer of productive labour, and conceive of productive labour in a broader sense than Marx did within the matrix of the capitalist valorisation process.

Much — very much — of what is now said about 'right' and 'left' and about the different colours within the Green party — as if we now had to bring the class struggle into the Green party in a kind of substitutionist way, since we can't wage it in the wider field outside — falls victim to a crude error that is spread by a number of interested parties: a confusion between the ideological divisions that are introduced among working people by the presently dominant relations, and the actual class division proper. At the very least, the error confuses strata within the working people with the dividing line between the people and the bourgeoisie in the broadest sense, which itself is not quite so easy to draw as it might seem.

There are of course people in the Green party who really do belong to the bourgeois middle class, who to some degree or other are businessmen, e.g. publishers, doctors, lawyers. The boundary lines are fluid here. So far, since I'm not employed anywhere and am living off the income from books that I wrote, incidentally, in the GDR, I should presumably count myself among this statistic. It is very probable that at present these people have a disproportionate influence, which again is certainly not independent of their privileged position, this being apparent already in their educational advantage. But this section is not characteristic of the mass base of the Green party. And class membership, moreover, says next to nothing as to the actual role people play in a movement that transcends existing conditions altogether — unless we still have the decisive street battle in mind. I would rather recall how Marx and Engels explained their own transition to the other side in the *Communist Manifesto* — 'at times when the class struggle reaches its decisive hour' — whatever might be concretely understood by a high point such as this. Today the pressure to take a stand is greater than ever before. People talk of petty-bourgeois elements. Who is it that's speaking? 'It's always other people who're philistines,' as Tucholsky put it. There is no purpose in raising our eyebrows because in our still bourgeois society there are people who are also bourgeois in the psychological sense — and this in all social classes. That is precisely the problem. Given how the traditional workers' movement has got stuck in bourgeois society, a new approach is indicated, one which can step out beyond the framework of this society, and as I see it, can also carry with it the workers as human beings.

It goes without saying that this hope transcends the context of a political party in the narrow sense. I am speaking above all of the ecology *movement*, whose tendency to develop a characteristic world-view I would assess as something positive. It is not just ecology that is moving people. This is only where the pressing material impulse comes from. What people really want is the next step forward to freedom; the threatening catastrophe is just the initial stimulus for this. It should not bother us that many people clothe this with the words 'and deliver us from evil' or 'thy kingdom come'. When Hegel and Hölderlin, both enthused by the French revolution, parted after studying in Tübingen, they said farewell with the imperative: 'God's kingdom!' What they *meant*, each of us can supply for themselves.

From rot und grün, *March 1980*

Beyond the Old Fronts

The balance of social forces that we have to shift is one of political psychology, with far more factors entering into it than can be directly derived from 'class position'. And for this reason I should like to make a confession, in order to take the bull by the horns as it were. I have a deliberately positive attitude towards what strictly rationalist thinkers probably label 'mysticism', which I am sometimes reproached with because in some comrades' opinion I pay too little attention to the different social interests. I am interested in the forces for cultural revolution that lie, in no small way, in Christ, Buddha and Lao Tzu. Forces that have made history. We need the gnostic tradition — as one aspect, not to fill the whole of life. I have long been drawn to such thinkers as Joachim di Fiore, Meister Eckhart, Spinoza and Pascal on account of the affinity of their mysticism to real freedom, which remains incomplete as long as it does not also include freedom of the spirit. I recently read that someone discovered a mystical experience of the young Marx, which would then be analogous to Luther's experience in the tower. I can well see this as possible. Taken realistically, mysticism, at least clear-headed mysticism, means a profound mobilisation of emancipatory forces in the human psyche, a phenomenon that has nothing other-worldly about it, and should be made accessible to everyone, for example by a practice of meditation. Even this, or precisely this, was formerly a privilege for the few. I believe that my position on this question was also that of Ernst Bloch.

As far as the questionable passages in the writings of Herbert Gruhl and Wolfgang Harich are concerned, are they the only people who bring with them elements of their background — the one from this social order, the other from the social order over there?[17] Just as Comrade Rabehl, for example, found me to be a crypto-Leninist who represents the stratum of specialists.[18] All right, the anti-authoritarian camp has at least learned that you don't get rid of what you want to negate just by taking an intellectual distance from it. Out through the door, and back again through the window. It is something quite different that I find interesting about mysticism. If Herbert Gruhl vacillates on the question of an 'authoritarian solution', this is a function of the doubt he expresses as to whether a voluntary consensus is attainable. If I remember correctly, he says that he does not see the new faith which could supply sufficient cohesive force to make a general agreement over values and goals possible. Previous cultural revolutions, at least as I have read about them in the various branches of world history, were always accompanied by an ideological synthesis with religious force. The question is one of the *quality* of our appeal, and of course not least its *contemporary* form, since we do not have to turn back the clock on two thousand years of intellectual progress, but precisely to make use of this. What we need today is the supersession of religion, in the well-known Hegelian sense, a supersession of religion for free people who do not throw themselves at anyone's feet. What I have in mind here is rather like Erich Fromm's position.

As far as the possible abuse of the corresponding human needs goes, the question is simply *which* powers are to prevail when the struggle for hearts and minds is decided in social practice. If, in view of the possibility that even an absolutely necessary transformation in culture can have an authoritarian outcome, *we* cultivate our scepticism and only see the dangers, we shall simply leave the field clear for the false prophet to gather his chosen people undisturbed.

How Do We Win Hegemony?

We must win people away from the other bloc, the right-conservative bloc, and change the bloc of reforming forces from within in such a way that it embarks as a whole on the path of a fundamental change of system — the 'third way' that has often been invoked, and leads forward from capitalism while at the same time avoiding the despotic apparatus state which for the developed countries is simply an unhistorical detour. This 'third way' is nothing other than the road to socialism, ever newly awaited, in the form appropriate to our tradition.

The Social-Democrat party in its present form will not open the way; the dual strategy of the Young Socialists is incompatible with the imprisonment of this party to the state which has long been internalised by its entire organism. The party of Helmut Schmidt can in no way call on the masses. The left in the SPD thus necessarily needs help from outside.

How do things stand with the historic compromise? In the first place, this is a Latin and especially an Italian affair. It seems to presuppose the existence of mass Eurocommunist and socialist parties. And on the other hand, if the Christian-Democrats as such are not an ally (and any tendency in this direction is the perversion of a fruitful idea),then at least the Catholic masses are, and the object is to alienate them from their party allegiance. The SPD as such cannot be the subject of a historic compromise that would lead beyond existing conditions in the way the Italian Communist Party would like. And the perspective of a grand coalition, which might also be derived from the Italian analogy, is still less suited to the political landscape that we would like to see in Germany.

But people often stick too close to the surface of things. Berlinguer drew a general political conclusion from the consideration that the workers' movement might be defeated in an attempt to capture the fortress frontally from its minority position by attack or counter-attack: not to rely on the intensification of internal class contradictions of the traditional kind. And he did so, of course, not least in view of the unavoidable experience that the dynamic of these class contradictions, taken as a whole, has a declining potential for shattering the system. The consequence is a neo-reformism, which has so far been discovered pragmatically rather than being based in theory, and is thus exposed to the danger of falling back into the old social-democratic gradualism. This is how I see it, other comrades may assess things differently.

Set against its background, however, I see the historic compromise as an exceedingly fruitful strategic project. Its key point is the idea of a great amalgamation, an alliance of 'all forces of work and culture' that is not just mechanical, but integral. This formula, as I see it, exactly corresponds to the concept of the collective worker, which tends to spread across the frontiers between classes, including individuals who despite their different class ascription are chiefly productive and constructive, not parasitical, and not increasing the sum of decay and jeopardy in the Italian social body. For the ultimate background to the historic compromise is of course the fact that in Italy, with its North-South gradient,the internal and external contradictions of capitalism are tangled together in a really vicious Gordian knot. What have the Italian workers to win if they are unable to break through in the direction of the traditional proletarian general solution, while the entire economy, the whole national life, is disintegrating because of a stalemate between the political forces? In which of the developed capitalist countries does the left as it stands and with its particular mentality have the prospect of winning more than 50 per cent support, and this even though the overwhelming majority of the population belong socially and economically to the oppressed and the exploited?

The answer is a historic compromise that transcends the old divisions to set in motion an overwhelming majority for the peaceful conquest of the state machine in all its levels and departments. The essence of this strategy is not class collaboration. The aim of the operation is to expel from the state machine all the old and exhausted forces, to transform the state machine, to clip off its parasitic and repressive members and thus make it, suitably sanitised, into the general instrument of a rational administration that no longer operates in the mode of domination. In traditional terms, this is a strategy for a war of position, a wearying situation of dual power even — and precisely — on the field of the state apparatus, which is kept going by millions of working people. If this apparatus is no longer just ascribed en bloc to the other side, if it is not relinquished to the unmitigated structural violence of capital reproduction and the direct influence of monopoly lobbies of all kinds, it can gradually become the instrument of social control, of incisive interventions into the sovereignty of capital, since the capital centralised in the state apparatus can then be used against the capital of the corporations. This is an idea worth developing beyond the Italian and Eurocommunist context.

A Possibility for West Germany

In the Federal Republic it is possible that factors which have previously found expression in a specific weakness of the left could now in fact offer an opportunity. The Italian Communist Party suffers, so to speak, from the fact that the contradictions which in the Federal Republic are now to be decided between the Social-Democrats and the Greens (in so far as the socialists to the left of the SPD understand their role), have in Italy to be waged in its midst. The PCI is prevented from a bold development of the new strategy precisely by its commitment to traditional working-class interests. We could even say that it does not have the opportunity to experiment first of all with the historic compromise on a smaller scale, and to practise and promote from this standpoint the supersession of traditional working-class interests into a more general concept of emancipation, in which these interests must in no way be lost sight of.

Sociologically, according to the traditional class structure, the Greens are still very unevenly represented in the different lines of the political spectrum. In general, their membership is dominated by younger people, who are presumably less advanced in their careers. Among them, as the SPD complains, are precisely those forces who ten years ago voted full of hope for the Social-Democrats. I see the whole political-psychological spectrum represented in the Green movement — i.e. conservatives (at least those concerned with the conservation of values rather than structures), democratic Christians, alternative liberals, democratic socialists — with these characteristics often cutting across each another in one and the same individual. If we manage to achieve a genuine communication in the new party, we shall soon stop thinking in terms of the labels people pin on themselves while they still need to be distinguished from a distance, rather than from close up.

I see the overall configuration as follows. Up till now we have a balance of forces with a good 50 per cent in the conservative camp and not quite 50 per cent in the camp of reform — if the Free-Democrat supporters are divided between the two. It may be that initially the socialist-liberal coalition was more favourable from our point of view. Qualitatively, however, the potential for reform will not really achieve anything until it is radicalised by a mass movement, and aims at radical reforms with a system-changing content.

From our standpoint, the Greens now offer a double opportunity. First, and precisely because of their heterogenous origin, even people who previously voted for the Christian-Democrats or the Free-Democrats can find a place in the forces of reform if they are seeking an alternative to their traditional political allegiance, whether they have been doing so for a long while or only recently. These are people to whom we should scarcely gain any direct access with a left socialist party, for example, partly because we ourselves have a false and restricted conception of our own identity. In this respect we have something to learn from the Greens. Whereas previously we could only hope in our debate with the SPD to shift the frontiers a little within one and the same reform potential, the Greens may well signify, in a somewhat longer timescale, the opportunity of achieving a significant numerical predominance for the reforming forces as a whole.

Secondly, with the Greens we can put the SPD and trade-union bureaucracy under pressure from two sides, and offer the left and Green forces within the Social-Democrat party and the trade unions a real stimulus and solidarity. The result of this would be precisely to effect the radicalisation of the reform potential mentioned above, eventually a predominance for the forces who stand for fundamental change in our living and economic arrangements, and seek to put an end to the rule of profiteering, the destruction of nature, human alienation and self-alienation.

From rot und grün, *March 1980*

A New Direction for the Totality

It is possible to dispute whether humanity has a goal. Perhaps. I think yes. One thing is certain, however, and far more important: the individual human being has a goal, no matter whether this is pursued deliberately or not. First of all, and beyond good or evil, this goal is a task that is in part inherited, in part acquired by education — to positively *live out* our species nature, our particular genotype, our character. This is a human characteristic. If a seed is destined to become a tall tree — given that it contains this tree within it — yet it only grows into a deformed dwarf because circumstances are unfavourable, it would feel the non-fulfilment of its destiny as *unhappiness* if it could reflect on it. Tagore puts it something like this.

There has never been so much unhappiness as there is today in the rich countries — anxiety, discontent, loneliness either with or without other people, failure and alienation of every kind — not even in the darkest and most impoverished of times. True, there have never been so many people; but that is not what I have in mind. Of each hundred people, more are now unhappy than ever before — with the possible exception of certain generations in the late imperial era of the single metropolis of Rome. To put it more accurately: there is more unhappy *consciousness*, more consciousness of being unhappy, than ever before.

The cause of this is first of all a positive one. In other words more 'subjectivity' (more individuality, more sense of self, more need for self-realisation) is initiated (even if it does not grow to fruition). And then most of the claims bound up with this are disappointed. All the more so, in that today everyone imagines they need everything. If not quite like Faust — down to the Mothers and up to God himself[19] — everyone would at least like to have the full wealth and width of a Faustian life, to range through the whole department store. This is bound up with Goethe's 'seed or husk'. Worst, however, is how many people fail even to reach a closed husk under the flood of externally-determined impulses.

How few indeed reach the beginning of a self-determined action which alone can give spiritual happiness. Not too much ego but too little, too little subjectivity.

What is the real reason why our successes bring us unhappiness, even the success expressed in all this wealth? In the last instance, it is not the individual person's fault if they fail to reach their goal. This lies rather in the human being as 'ensemble of social relations'. The 'objective dialectic', the 'historical necessity' that has led us into civilisation, to high culture, must have a *fault* in it: a fault in relation to the natural claim of the individual to freedom, love and happiness — and thus to a life without too much fear.

'World history is not the place of happiness', so Hegel taught, and his doctrine is rooted deeper in all of us (not only us Marxists) than we are aware. It is a defeatist doctrine. True as it is at a distance, we could not live according to such a precept even if our physical existence were compatible with it. But as things stand today, we shall only survive at all if, in all our understanding, we go beyond the idea that freedom is nothing but the understanding of necessity. The ascent of a species and its decline are both equally necessary, as long as we are thinking in terms of the *spontaneous* process of natural history. If a swarm of locusts multiplies limitlessly in favourable conditions, and then falls upon a stretch of land and eats it bare until the basis of its own existence is consumed and it perishes, this is also a law-like and necessary process. We shall probably meet the same fate, if we do not take far more seriously what Marx had to say on this point and make a *leap* into the realm of freedom.

What Marx did not yet see, as we can see it today, is that we cannot simply raise ourselves above the realm of necessity (of production, etc.) *as it presently is*. This is a foundation which, in the law-like form in which it arose, cannot bear what we must attempt if we are to *survive in happiness*. We must accordingly study Marx's historical materialism, precisely because it correctly describes the course of history up till now, in the same way that the clever capitalists studied Marx's *Capital*: to look for the gaps in the laws discovered, in order to clear the ways that promise us a future. The question really is one of breaking the continuity of history. And this, in my view, means mobilising the human being as an *individual*, using our awareness of unhappiness as a springboard to opening a new path for the human being as 'ensemble of social relations'.

The entire material world around us, the whole pseudo-universe of institutions we have constructed, shows a prevailing tendency towards death and decay. But these things did not exist at the time our human *nature* was being formed, in the millions of years and especially in the 30,000 years before homo sapiens entered the age of high culture and a culture of domination. (These institutions are *less* necessary.) If we remain mere cogs in their works, it will soon be all over for us. Let's therefore seek to give the totality a new direction. Let's *subordinate* wealth and the institutions to the human genotype, so that everything positively returns to this, just as it proceeded from it and still does proceed from it. Historical relativism is today outmoded, given that it does not see human nature or nature in general as signifying any indispensable norm, since even unnatural forms of society can evidently make history too.

Moreover, we have to oppose ourselves to the Moloch, *no matter how great it is*. We could only drop out if there was a second world to drop into. We have to achieve a counterforce in this one world as it is. Such a counterforce requires in the first place its own alternative foundation, the gradual construction of a new context of life. Here Rudi Dutschke's slogan of a march through the institutions attains a new relevance. This 'walking on two legs', 'starting both at the top and at the bottom' is immediately comprehensible as a general principle. If it is not so comprehensible for many interested parties, this indicates our objective problem of standing at a new beginning, with still too little in the way of consolidated and enlightened forces, and with too little time — not just because of the timing of elections. I recommend therefore the Gramscian attitude: 'Scepticism with the intellect, optimism with the will!'

Original text of an article in Pardon, *April 1980*

To Change the World through Faith

I argued for scepticism with the intellect, optimism with the will. In this connection I have already experienced on more than one occasion that it is seen as somewhat impudent to believe in the possibility of changing the world for the better. 'Where is he (still) living, then!' In any case, there is a widespread doubt as to whether there is any possibility of avoiding the threatening total catastrophe.

There is the 'overkill' that the strategists of both sides prepare against each other, and which has a greater probability of falling on us the more we base our 'security' upon it.

There is the polarisation of wealth and poverty in the North-South conflict, on a scale completely determined by ourselves, which will lead in a short space of time to the starvation of half a billion human beings.

There is our voracious production machine, driven by the pressure to turn money into more money and by the concern to give this business a social guarantee, a machine which is eating even more rapidly into the mountain of resources the smaller this becomes, and casting its debris to the poles, into the stratosphere, into the bowels of the earth, and right into the future as well.

This gigantic mechanism seems to run more or less automatically. We are so accustomed to the little conveniences with which the great evil rolls towards us. We 'need' everything the market has to offer, because we are supposed to need it so that the whole clockwork can turn quicker and quicker. Of course there is no way we can change anything, simple people that we all are in relation to it.

What we can rely on once and for all, however, is that the final upshot of all this depends chiefly on us.

Those 'in charge', in other words, will not put on the brakes. We may think this is because they do not want to. And there are indeed such people. One of them is already hard at work. And another still worse one is waiting in the wings. But this in itself does not matter. Without us, without the most pressing impulse from 'below', none of those 'in charge' could do any differently, even if they wanted to.

Willy Brandt, with the report of his North-South commission, how much more powerful is he really than any other Willy in this country when it comes to those things that really matter, the question of the basic direction of the totality? No one in this position can do any good so long as there are too few people who do not want to change not only objective conditions but also their own lives, and this in a quite basic way. We shall have to change fundamentally, if the South is to be freed from the model that is tailored for it here.

We shall also have to take risks. It is one thing to refuse to have nuclear power stations on our doorstep. This suggests itself easily enough. But we still have to supply these to Brazil, if not to other countries where this is still more absurd. Just think of the jobs in our export industries. Otherwise we should run the greatest risk, that of changing our whole system. Since this is a question of jobs, there's nothing we can do about it. That would be up to our capitalists.

As long as we proceed in this way, what we really want is to leave those 'in charge' just as they are. In particular, we want Schmidt and not even Brandt, who sometimes still has impractical ideas. Carry on with Schmidt, carry on with overkill, carry on with increasing per capita income (the poor have only themselves to blame, in the last instance, if they lag behind our efficiency). Carry on with 100 mph. on the motorways, with the electric meter outside the back door, above all carry on in the direction laid down. The economic order, the whole institutional heaven, tells us to.

If we want to change something, it must really be the system as a whole. We must force it into a completely different mould. Who is to carry out this simple task? Simple people? Indeed simple people, since there is no one else. To do this, they must first of all give themselves a different mould, collectively as well. Why not the mould of a mass movement that is unpolitical and unskilled — in relation to the prevailing level of politics and expertise? Its prospects depend on the strength of the impulse, on the pull of the promised future. Formerly this was called faith. It is something that is mentally completely real, completely within the human spirit: the highest level of an optimism of the will.

If something of this nature takes hold on a mass scale, the new order may begin in a seemingly ludicrous way. If ever there was a false start in terms of the customary standards, a ridiculous uprising devoid of prospects and undertaken in bad company — with the simplest of people — it was that of a certain Jesus of Nazareth. And yet he is still spoken of today, two thousand years later, and there again seem to be more people who care to follow him, or rather, to follow the principle he embodied. So this was not completely unsuccessful. What Jesus once said to the patient he healed was true of Jesus himself: 'Your faith has saved you.'

There is clearly a law-like connection between the degree of the danger and the mobilisation of human impulse. It is one of humanity's experiences that whenever the writing is on the wall for a particular age, a new awakening takes place. To change the world through faith. Marx had his faith too. And as this is not yet spent, his reference to the necessary illusions without which nothing better ever comes about is still valid today.

Original text of an article in Pardon, *May 1980*

The Bloc in Power, the New Historic Bloc, and the Problem of the Left

On the Constellation of the 1980s

(...) The first thing that seems clear to me is that since 1974-75 a further stage of capitalism that began after the Second World War has come to an end. Previously capital has managed again and again to conduct a forward flight — contrary to our assessments at the time — since behind every threshold that it crossed in the form of crisis it found qualitatively new possibilities of expansion waiting for it. This time that seems no longer to be the case, this time a new 'redivision of the world' at a stage Lenin did not foresee really does seem to be 'excluded'. Not excluded in terms of the market: it could still provide billions of people with Volkswagens and perhaps even private planes if this were materially possible. It would however be materially impossible to give all the six, eight or ten billion human beings that there might be in a short space of time even the same per capita consumption of raw materials and energy achieved by countries like the GDR and Czechoslovakia, for example, which are seen by many people here as going short.

There can thus be no question of continuing this type of expansion of production and needs. The field that capital can plough is coming to an end, yet capital is expansionist by its innermost nature. At present productivity per worker is making a new leap forward, driven on by the same greed for profit. We shall really have to need private planes, so that a lot more steel etc. can be produced and no jobs be 'lost' in the steel industry. (The word 'lost' shows how we socialists are trapped by the logic of capital.)

The stability of the prevailing power relations depends in a variety of ways on the rate of growth. But today this is no longer held back simply by the blockages inherent to the capitalist valorisation process. The increasing scarcity of raw materials is having its restricting effect on growth, first of all economically, through rising prices, but soon also as an absolute material limit. It is precisely through the scarcity of resources that the North-South conflict has started to press itself into the consciousness of people here, i.e. not primarily out of motivations of solidarity. If the USA is able for a while to supply its needs from its own territory, i.e. for a few decades, the same is not true for Western Europe or Japan. This is also leading to increasing conflicts of interest between the three late-capitalist zones. In the capitalist metropolises, with their dependence on raw materials, we shall experience the development of a similar political-psychological siege mentality, whipped up by the reactionaries, as we see today in Israel or white South Africa. Popular reaction to the revolution in Iran and its consequences, incited by the West European mass media and still more so by the American, give a foretaste of what is possible. Psychological preparations for war are already gaining new ground.

The victory of tendencies such as this becomes more probable with every year that the policy of growth continues. It cannot be halted simply by political defence measures — and it is impossible to pose the question in broader terms if every four years people are simply recommended to choose the lesser evil. If the production machine along with its entire dependent structure of goods and needs is not fundamentally reconstructed and an ever greater section of the population motivated to this end, then the dilemma is inescapable, and we shall face the political consequences in the shape of authoritarian solutions.

A far-sighted alternative must therefore settle in good time on a movement of *conversion*[20] which aims at nothing less than the reconstruction of our civilisation right down to its material foundations. This requires a combination of two lines of struggle: against the driving and regulatory mechanism of monopoly competition for maximum profits *and* against the other side of this mechanism — the structure of human need as governed by the compulsion to realise capitalist mass production on the market.

The question of growth divides even socialists. If we insist, given otherwise unchanged assumptions — i.e. the existing balance of forces — that the immediate needs of the wage-earners should have priority, then we are simply one additional factor keeping everything going on as before. No matter how orthodox and revolutionary our arguments may sound, we are simply helping to reproduce the present system on an expanded scale. We are playing a dependent part within the system. Nothing can be done without a change in priorities. The short-term interests that prevailing conditions dictate to people in their capacity as wage-earners stand in a very real conflict to their own long-term interests.

History to date offers only two models of resolving such profound conflicts. Something along the lines of Plato's Republic with its guardians, which today means a super-bureaucratic dictatorship, or else a social-revolutionary mass movement with its sights on some future goal. And this is what we must set our sights on. The majority required for fundamental changes can only come about through a political mass movement of this type. Those who take part in it, just like the majority of supposedly middle-class ecologists today, will continue to have their particular interests as wage-earners, as long as we have not yet achieved a new economic order. But the conflict of labour and capital will not provide the movement's mobilising force, since in our part of the world capitalist exploitation as such is no longer the decisive existential challenge to which people have to respond.

The energy needed to venture upon such a leap can only be mobilised by a movement that represents an entire world-view. The question facing us is not whether we like this or not, but rather how we should act and what we can do in order to give the emotions released the most rational direction possible. Ecological humanism, continuing the tradition of the Enlightenment, is a proposed description that can well be used here. It includes the demand for the general emancipation of all human beings — men and women.

The Shifts in the Domestic Balance of Forces

The weakness of the opposition forces in the Federal Republic up to now is a handicap to progressive developments throughout Europe. Yet there is no prospect of solving the problem in such a way that the left in its traditional form gains the same kind of influence as it has for example in the Latin countries. And what would be gained by this in the long run anyway? Doesn't the situation of the left there also have its inherent limitations? There are many countries indeed where the difficulties are greater than they are here! Not only has the traditional workers' movement in its economic struggle turned out to be a formation within the pattern bourgeois society has adopted, but so has the left in the political sense. We shall not reach our goal if we want to catch up with something that our national history has not provided. The low level of traditional politicisation in this country offers us the specific opportunity of making a new beginning. The present mobilisation is based on existential footholds that cannot be understood in terms of traditional political or economic doctrine. This means that 'left' and 'socialist' self-conceptions and models of behaviour are mentalities that no longer suffice, but must be qualitatively further developed. Separate left socialist parties of the conventional type, to the 'left' of the major party of the traditional workers' movement and clamouring for the restoration of earlier goals, may well take their stand on lost positions and can easily have a retarding effect, tying forces to superseded lines of conflict devoid of prospects. The idea of a separate left alternative in the Federal elections belongs to a perspective oriented to the past. It will probably lead ultimately to a recommendation to vote for Schmidt, and this means for the best man of the ruling bloc.

As far as terminology is concerned, the concept of a bloc denotes a combination of social interests with respect to the political-psychological balance of forces. It assumes a more or less clear line of division between various basic attitudes towards social change. It always gains importance in crises of transition, in times of rapid social and cultural flux. Such blocs in domestic politics are the expression of what could be called 'historic parties'. These are based, in other words, on the political-psychological division between progressive, conservative and reactionary forces that recurs in various historic epochs. To change the world; to leave everything as it is, with minor improvements; to turn the clock back — these basic attitudes then constitute political parties. It goes without saying that economic interests play a part in the decisions individuals make. But no matter that certain tendencies may be distinguished at the statistical level, it is clear that one and the same class position presents a range of options, just as different class positions can meet up in the same option. Above all, specific class interests, which always exist in relation to those of another class, have a varying importance at different times even in their contribution to the overall material interest of the individuals concerned. If, as happened for example with the Christian movement under the Roman empire, masses of people came together across class divisions, we must concede — if we are to remain historical materialists in our method — that in the last analysis there were real concrete interests that accounted for this. Even these Christians had to live.

It goes without saying that class membership always has an influence in determining allegiance to political parties. But whenever the struggle of the principal classes in a social formation is not the most important source of social development — and there are indeed times such as this — class membership is not decisive for the individuals' choice of party, and thus also not decisive for the character of this party.

At present, in fact, even the traditional concepts used to characterise these 'historic parties' seem strangely confused, since we need a change in the world that goes against much of what was formerly seen as progress, and we have to maintain and restore much that has historically been lost. The 'historic parties' can thus be reduced to really only two. One of these, accustomed to all kinds of privilege and enjoyment of power, wants to keep everything going on as before. We can call this the bloc of forces of stability, the forces of inertia. Inert continuation along the same lines. Even a speed limit on the motorway is too much for them: 'Free motoring for free citizens!' This is the party that executes the 'compulsion of things', through which the world will perish without any chance of salvation.

The other 'party', the bloc of reform, wants 'to change everything radically, so that everything will remain as it is', in the words of the wise Sicilian aristocrat Lampedusa.[21] This aphorism with its conservative note is very useful today, in as much as it most likely characterises the motivation of the majority of people at present involved in the Green movement. We can rely on it that with such a radical transformation not *everything* will remain as it is, and other people certainly don't rule this out either.

The class interests of monopoly capital and the structural inertia of the bureaucratic state machine combine to form the vital nerve of the bloc in power, which includes the cartel of established parties. These parties are distinguished only with respect to the relative permeability they offer to the opposing interests which find expression in the new historic bloc. This idea means among other things that people in the established parties, and especially of course in the SPD — though not only there — need not be more or less automatically classed as part of the ruling bloc. The same goes for people in the state apparatus and even for capitalist managers, including individual businessmen. At times like this there have always been countless people of this or that rank in society who have taken off what Marx called their economic character-masks. (Sava Morozov helped finance the Russian revolution.)[22]

The bloc in power also incorporates countless people who by their class position should not have any interest, or hardly any, in the unchanged perpetuation or extension of the existing situation, but do so out of certain needs, fears, etc. that operate in a complex fashion.

On the other hand, the bloc of reform — which is at present only embryonic and just beginning to encroach into the human potential still available to the established parties — is only semi-conscious of its alternative mission. Commitment to it is often still directed very much at particulars, at small segments, whereas we shall be forced to examine our entire lives.

Those commentators who point to the 'former' activities of many people involved in the new movement are reading the signs back to front: these 'former' people are the forerunners of a massive escape from the ties of the established parties which are decaying and falling apart, from the established party system in general. All three major parties belong to a past era. We can see the general tendency of a long-run strengthening of alternative positions both outside the traditional parties and in the first instance within them as well. I was less than precise in the special issue of *rot and grün* when I classed the entire potential represented by the SPD in the bloc of reform;[23] for there are of course strong elements within this party which taken in isolation belong to the bloc of inertia, just as the SPD does in its capacity as a governing party. The same is true of the trade unions.

Today the dividing line does not only run between people, but frequently also within them. Scarcely anyone is completely 'old', scarcely anyone completely 'new'. Often even comrades who see themselves as left of the SPD think and act partly in such a way that the result is to reproduce the existing conditions rather than transcend them. Backsliding of this kind happens to all of us — most commonly if we are attacked and do not have an adequate answer to hand. We should look out for signs of this in one another. In the last analysis, it is not a question of unavoidable individual mistakes, but rather of our line of conduct in general. In a situation of radical change it is advantageous both to individuals and to the cause to encourage relaxed discussion, experiment, and candid searching. I am certain that the realignment and regrouping of forces leading to their crystallisation in these two blocs has already begun, and for reasons that are historically comprehensible it is especially strong here in the Federal Republic of Germany, where the traditional and now outdated basic structures of political life in bourgeois society are less deeply rooted in people's behaviour.

We must not ignore the combination of various particular class and sectional interests which is met within each bloc. Historic fronts are no longer formed only along the divisions of class interest. This means that even for the bloc in power, the capitalist class interest in the narrower sense is no longer the sole constitutive factor, just as the power politics of the Roman empire cannot be attributed simply to the interests of the traditional ruling class that grew up in the republican era. Of course, the main line in the spectrum of interest for the bloc that seeks to perpetuate the existing conditions still lies very close to the traditional interest of the bourgeoisie. In the reforming bloc, the shift from specific class interest to the interest of general human emancipation is far greater.

We find ourselves in a strategic situation, at a real crossroads of history, not only in the Federal Republic, though here in particular. The Green movement could become a political contribution of European significance that our country can make. It may be that in the last third of this century what is developing in the countries of late capitalism is no longer — as before — a mere theory, but an actual consciousness of general crisis, a crisis of all relations of life. This points the way out of existing conditions in a different and indeed a more comprehensive fashion than does the actual class consciousness of the workers. It is developed first of all by the more intellectualised strata, but it radiates out from here into all other social milieus, and in no way comes to a halt at the factory gates. It thus raises afresh the question of how we are to find a way out of capitalism, and this time in an optimistic perspective.

A Crucial Decision for the Left

The cardinal question for us, then, is whether we intend to stand for the perpetuation of the existing political-psychological structure, or for its fundamental transformation. If we simply define ourselves as to the left of the SPD, or as the left within the SPD, and try as we formerly did to have an influence from this position on the traditional workers' movement, this means working to preserve the existing structure, condemning ourselves to a declining effectiveness and looking ahead to a weakening of the whole reforming camp. It is only from such a perspective that I can explain how the planned Socialist Conference can be viewed as an 'emergency discussion on the rapidly changing and deteriorating state of the left'. Then it is only consistent to confine yourself in every respect to the defence of existing positions and effectively give your blessing to the existing political-psychological structure. Warnings against the 'bloc in power' actually have a demobilising character, if they are only intended as protest and defence. People don't like having to move on, they don't like having to leave behind the thin protecting wall of their encampment.

I recently read a very stimulating article by Ernst Köhler on 'Some Timorous Objections Against Left-Wing Pessimism'.[24] He draws attention to a current in German history which we try either to conceal or else to accentuate in a negative manner. Köhler's approach becomes still more interesting when you remember in reading it that a very similar constellation, the depoliticisation of the masses in the universal state of Hellenistic Rome, was one of the decisive preconditions for the rise of Christianity, which originally was not a political movement but a movement of cultural regeneration, though of course it ultimately became political. Today the cultural alternative very swiftly leads to political articulation. What in Köhler's essay seems partly an impending reality, and partly emerges as a task, can be formulated as the 'politicisation of German subjectivity'. If we are convinced that this can only express itself in a reactionary way, then we remain in a state of defensive resignation.

Although we all think that conditions here must somehow be changed, too many of us still do not believe, or no longer believe, that anything can be done to bring about this change. It is precisely because I do believe we can do something, that we can at least make a great contribution to change, that I am ready to take a lot of practical risks, and any theoretical risk, as far as the search for new ways forward is concerned. I get reproachful references to the power structure that we have to deal with: that it's there, that it functions well, that the hydra has innumerable heads. Sure. But doesn't this warning have a defeatist purpose? Not to try anything? To curl up like a hedgehog and protect ourselves? The left, the radical democrats, etc. have always been defeated in Germany — why shouldn't this just happen once again? People are haunted by fears, and who but the reactionaries can give them political confirmation? In my view we can do the bloc in power no greater service than sing this song, to the tune of the *Winterreise*.[25]

At the Karlsruhe congress I myself spoke of the Strauss danger. It seems sufficiently clear to me that we reject him, and why we reject him. But it is not particularly productive to speak so much about what we are against. And there is another interest concerned that we should limit ourselves to this. More foresight in this old game instead of too much foresight in the new game! It is also not good to mystify the opponent. He is a man who has probably already passed his peak, and his actual room for manoeuvre, in the not very likely case that he should become Chancellor, would in no way be independent of the strength of the democratic mobilisation against him. Satire and exposure, moreover, do not change the world enough. The Romans in their *Satyricon* had only the reflection of their decay, not any alternative. We shall do no better with a hostile image of Strauss. Against the undeniable danger of Strauss we should rather put forward our positive programme. This would be one which would still get through to the Christian-Democrat rank and file after the election, especially then, and not only to the followers of those parties closer to us. Strauss is now saying a lot of things, for example against too much state intervention, which can be used against himself. He would find it difficult the next time round with his own electors if all those tendencies which he now blames on the socialist-liberal coalition were to continue and become even more pronounced under his aegis. He would not be able to conduct such an effective government as the clever Helmut Schmidt. At a time that is politically difficult for capital, since the falling rate of profit does not permit the former level of bribery, Schmidt is in a better position to provide the sovereigns of big business with the class peace they require. The masters of the banks and corporations do not have such a pressing need for Strauss, they are not even so very keen on him.

If you think in longer terms than the coming election, it becomes still more clear that we must use the present time to build up opposing forces, i.e. to extend the catchment area of alternative politics to new people. There is a danger in the overall situation of the rich late-capitalist countries that casts far greater shadows at the present time than Strauss does today. What will happen in domestic politics if the struggle for the ever dwindling supply of raw materials touches the arteries of our economic life? Then we are threatened with a fortress neurosis like that of Israel, or the white populations of Zimbabwe and South Africa. We have to work against this constellation on a broad front, not only in the narrower political sense, but above all by changing our own mode of production and way of life in good time.

Mere defence against Strauss, let alone an anxiety psychosis, is not by itself politics. If we confine ourselves to trying to prevent Strauss, we remain trapped by the logic of the ruling bloc. The danger that Strauss might expel us from our positions in the universities is a consideration that, as I see it, we can only allow a subordinate place in our thoughts. In the long run we cannot achieve anything if we are not prepared to take risks when these are necessary. The offensive response would be the strongest preparation of alternative working and living situations, the expansion of the Network Initiatives designed to support individual projects, and which can also keep comrades above water if they are faced with hardship. We must keep our personal perspectives open, less with a view to any kind of direct persecution, which does not look overwhelmingly likely, but rather as regards dropping out and changing course. It will be a long march, not only through the institutions. No one can be quite sure where they will end up, how far this will lead them. We must be prepared.

In any case, the vote this autumn involves more than just opposition to Strauss, and more than the Green party in its present incomplete state. We need to give the signal for a far more comprehensive reorientation that can encompass the broadest strata of the population. This signal should not be postponed for another four years.

If it should become clear shortly before the Federal election that the attempt to break the undemocratic 5-per-cent barrier was doomed to failure, I would request that the left-wing Greens don't make a unilateral decision, but decide what to do together with the other forces involved. In certain circumstances there may be good reasons for continuing the campaign even then.

Tentative Remarks on the Socialist Identity

If the 5-per-cent barrier is giving rise to hesitation in many comrades, the reason doesn't lie so much in failures of analysis. Our problem is not one of theory, or only in so far as we see fidelity to certain principles as equivalent to fidelity to ourselves in general. The source of dogmatism is always that we are inclined to confuse our intentions with the formulations in which we originally expressed these. Naturally, in order to solve our problem we need new theory, since we need good reasons for overcoming the fixations rooted in our unconscious.

In my opinion, the prospects are more favourable than many of us think. The general tendency is a long-run strengthening of alternative positions both outside and within the existing parties, organisations, institutions, etc., i.e. in society in general. Discontent and a feeling of crisis are more widespread in society than they were ten years ago. It is likely that there are many more forces ready than ever before, since the left that got under way in the sixties is still being reinforced, if only slowly, from subsequent generations.

The erosion that is sometimes lamented affects only the specific positions developed in the last ten years, which have now proved to be in need of overhaul both conceptually and organisationally. In the Federal Republic of Germany we are particularly affected by what throughout Western Europe is known as the crisis of Marxism. For reasons that were in no way subjective, the Extra-Parliamentary Opposition of the 1960s took up its Marxism directly in the form of the original texts. As far as I can see, scarcely one facet of the variegated history of the socialist and workers' movement was lacking: almost every line was represented in the spectrum of the left. Events that had happened successively since the birth of Marxism were repeated in abbreviated form alongside one another: from German and West European social-democracy via Lenin to Stalin, Mao Zedong, Ho Chi Minh, Fidel Castro, Frantz Fanon. Only after this did the movement begin to 'return home' to contemporary Europe, by way of Gramsci.

Even if the reception of Marx at that time has not been analysed in detail, methodological considerations suggest that the entire subsequent history was already prefigured at the beginning, in the ghettoised character of the experiment and a reception of the rediscovered gospel governed by the search for an identity to be maintained against all official forces. I have been able to experience on two occasions in Hanover how thick the atmosphere at that time must have been. More than a few people must have had an experience similar to the first Pentecost. Things like this do not just happen for subjective reasons, not without a kind of mandate from a wider context. In other words, May 1968 in Paris, the highest expression of the upsurge of that time, was not accidental.

The students struck the first blow, as has happened often in modern history — and in Paris they already reached across to the young workers. Substituting for the slower-moving body of society as a whole, they gave voice to the general discontent which people experience in a society dominated by the rule of capital, as the inner driving motor of alienated large-scale technology, super-organisation and state bureaucracy, even in the midst of all those consumer goods for the sake of which they daily subjugate themselves. 'Imagination to power!' was a slogan of clear negation of everything that the apparatuses of legitimation hold dear, as the supposedly inescapable compulsion of things.

Has the impulse of May 1968 been lost, then? Certainly not in West Germany, at any rate. All that has been lost is the traditional formulation of the question of power. The awakening to the old goals under new conditions made use of the old theory for want of an adequate new one. Yet this old theory proved unsuited to the new constellation, and above all unsuited to the new social forces, who were thus led to a ritual of conjuring up the dead, i.e. the subject of revolution that had been formulated in a previous age. This was a wrong direction: even in the workers it did not really address the striving for emancipation — which today involves the worker more as an individual seeking personal development than as a class aiming at the collective exercise of power, with all the consequences this has so far brought with it.

The celebrated texts, though resuscitated in people's minds, did not come to grips with things politically, since they were oriented to a *form* of struggle that is no longer extant: primarily to political overthrow instead of primarily to cultural transformation. The student movement very soon brought to a political short-circuit the whole new approach which began at that time and which it was itself the first to express. This was the sole cause of its collapse, which was rapid enough, and it subsequently hurled itself into the regression of those anachronistic party foundations which, in Marx's expression, could become no more than a farce in this repetition of history. The disappointment with organisational models, and the obstacles that even the non-sectarian groups confront in this respect, only show that the new situation has still to be intellectually mastered.

Hence the resolute attempt to reconstruct the old Marxian 'class for itself'; hence the pains taken to excavate and intensify the 'buried class consciousness', inevitably attempted from outside. This in some ways reminds me of Khrushchev's 'restoration of Leninist norms'. Just as I am unsure whether the victory of the pre-war Social-Democrats would have led to better results than a 'bureaucratic workers' state', so I also think that the old recipes would not make us happy today even if they succeeded. Still less than in the non-capitalist world with its comparatively simple structure, a mere change in political power would not bring into being here a new society, a better civilisation and culture.

The course of events since 1968 gives us a practical response to the question as to where there has really been continuity: far more in cultural than in political phenomena! If imagination has failed to come to power, it has certainly not given up. The turn toward communism has continued. The ecology movement has got under way. The women's movement and other movements against the repression bound up with sex roles have made progress. In our country in particular, a large number of alternative projects and lifestyles have sprung up. The critical study of social conditions has made headway, so that we at least have reliable descriptions of how things stand, even if these are often more in the way of exposure, presenting the power of the structure as almost inescapable, rather than pointing forward as interventions. And last but not least, something has survived which we must now really release and make better use of: a culture of Marxist thought. In this respect, continuity was indeed seriously interrupted by the catastrophe of 1933-45 and its consequences. More has been restored in this respect than it is possible to read. Analyses have a higher level than the manipulation of theory in the interest of practical politics, where there is still a tendency for the dogmatic transfer of slogans, formulas and resolutions from quite different constellations. In any case, we now have the capacity to present the great majority of society with the sketch of a total alternative, at the various levels from a theoretical book through to a newspaper article or television commentary.

All that is needed, then, is to find the language for this, and the determination. I believe that at this moment we are not yet in a position to ascertain how far we are really prevented from doing this by repression, and how far we prevent ourselves. We could learn something here from the church and start with the simplest missionary practices (I don't mean fraudulent and manipulative ones), adapting ourselves to the mentality of our audience without abandoning the spirit of our message. I would see a concrete model for this in the statement of a French priest who, when asked what he sought for his church in the new Algeria, said that he hoped to help people become better Moslems. It should not take us so long to get down to our own task of taking what we have to offer to those people who in our opinion need it, and who we must allow the right to adapt it to their own requirements.

What Role for the Socialist Conference?

In the first place, the need for a unification of our forces has arisen from the crisis of our own organisations. But the impulse for a genuine enterprise in this direction is a response to the changed atmosphere of social development as expressed in the decline of the socialist-liberal coalition, the candidacy of Strauss, and above all and positively, in the Green movement. Just as important is the sharpening of the international situation. The idea that all socialist forces, the entire left whether organised — in whatever way — or unorganised, and no matter how they describe themselves, at least need to take counsel together, and that a forum must be provided for this, was already in the air. This was the background to my proposal.

With the Socialist Conference we should introduce a process of elaborating the theoretical projects needed for a genuine intervention in social development in the 1980s. We — that is everyone in our country who see themselves as 'left' or 'socialist', or still better, all those who are actively seeking the path that leads beyond capitalism towards the general emancipation of humanity — men and women. This position is less identical than it ever was with any particular party or group. Our effectiveness will depend in the first place on a new political orientation, and this means that our judgement of the situation should for a start approximate to the social reality. Questions of organisation have only a derivative importance in relation to this; organisational failure has almost always been the result of inappropriate points of departure and unrealistic perspectives.

We can take it that a large number of people who feel themselves on the left are urgently awaiting a rather more coherent and rounded practical orientation, as would already result from even an as yet incomplete consensus that transcends the various different standpoints. In this connection, the centre of gravity of such agreement has to lie in the analysis of the domestic and international situation, the assessment of lines of conflict and perspectives, the determining of points of attack for our activities, rather than in tactical considerations, let alone merely electoral ones. These latter are not unimportant, but it is clear that this is where there can be least initial unity, and we definitely want to avoid cramping the discussion by starting out here. If the coming election has given us an impulse to accelerate our project, we should still not let our discussion be determined by this short-term horizon affecting only the political superstructure. Otherwise we would have to abandon the ideological initiative to the other side right from the start.

Since we have previously lacked such a forum for a dialogue in which our various organisations, groups, tendencies, wings of parties, etc. could all join in, at least on this large scale, the very fact that the Socialist Conference is being held will give a hopeful signal. The conference will also have at least the minimal effect, if all tendencies have the same right to speak and if all this is appropriately documented, of making known the different standpoints, i.e. showing outside the specific context of the groups where a particular line of argument coincides with other arguments that are similarly more or less well summarised. Since it is assumed that on some questions a polarisation may emerge, we should insist right from the start that the discussion be conducted in a spirit of solidarity. The irreconcilable style that Lenin successfully stamped on his party would certainly be quite unsuited to our situation and our tasks here today. On these assumptions, however, the clear confrontation of different positions would already be a most useful step forward,especially if this takes place in a broad context of discussion. It would help comrades throughout the country to make up their minds.

Yet our attempt should go beyond the comparison and confrontation of positions. All of us, no matter where we come from, should see ourselves not merely as representatives of particular organisations, groups, tendencies, wings of parties, but also let our individual standpoints come into play and seek agreement with other people. Where there are differences of opinion, this would mean above all making internal criticism wherever possible, instead of simple rejection and external confrontation. A third and very important effect could thus be the reciprocal understanding of other connections of ideas and their backgrounds of motivation, which can already open the way to a convergence and to further perspectives for discussion.

This would be the condition for a fourth possible effect, which would already signify an important success. If we could aim collectively at an advance in our theoretical assessment of conditions and in the quality of argument for our political conclusions, i.e. at grasping more exactly what is new in the situation and indicating more precisely the general context of action and corresponding goals for practical activities that are decided on either by groups or by individuals. At all events, the conference will present us more sharply with the problems that we all have to think about, and it will offer all comrades in the country who are interested footholds for their own considerations. Precisely in as much as it is not the assembly of a particular organisation, and promises to become more than the sum of its participants, we can develop its character as a place for purposeful communication, providing a wider-ranging framework of ideas and more firmly linking together the intellectual network. Since we do not have the compulsion to consensus that is encumbent on organisations, differences of opinion will not have a negative effect on solidarity, but will rather make contact more fruitful. As in scientific institutions, the necessary minimum of organisation would be completely subordinated to the process of intellectual work and the requirements of cooperation on particular projects.

We should also invite the participation of representatives from other forces concerned with fundamental changes, people who do not see themselves as socialists but have an interest in how we deal with problems to which they are scarcely less committed than we are ourselves.If it is true that in future people will divide more and more within the existing political formations, we must expressly make way for meetings across membership lines. In this way we can win people over. For those who have already opted for an alternative path, access to our conference and the ability to take part in its discussion should be a matter of course. I shall for example try and interest Herbert Gruhl in this (...)

The Left and the Greens

Marxist socialism with its original connection to the workers' movement is only one of the traditions linking up in the new mass movement now arising. Through the problems this movement tackles it presses beyond capitalism in a social-revolutionary direction. The very logic of their commitment will itself bring people involved to recognise that the roots of the ecology crisis lie in capitalism. The starting-point of their mobilisation is already that human beings need a different society by their very nature — which we Marxists have long taken as far too relative — and not simply in order to survive. Above all, our method of understanding history, our historical materialism, which has absolutely nothing in common with what many people reject as the 'materialism of our time', will prove a much needed instrument in sharpening the Green project. We can decisively help to ensure that the utopian aspect of the Green movement, which is a necessary aspect, is at the same time basically mediated with the realities of the situation, and that the cause does not become absolutised and hence absurd. It would certainly be useful for the common cause if we could get our partners, in so far as they are working on theory, to read Marx and Engels's *German Ideology* for once, before they confine themselves in their methodology to 'Feuerbachian man' and Feuerbachian 'love'.

The Socialist Conference could perhaps be the first step towards an Initiative of Democratic Socialists to be organised later, which would see itself as an alternative to the majority politics of the Social-Democratic party and — without binding recommendations to individual comrades — would orient itself towards work alongside or with the Green party, or at least with the ecology movement in the wider sense. This initiative would associate and combine its action right from the start with all other alternative forces. We could set ourselves the task of bringing the Marxist tradition, but also all other strands of socialist thought both old and new, into convergence on new and common positions.

For example, it would be a most urgent and also a rewarding task to bring the different attempts at a strategy of transformation in the key economic realm which are grouped under the heading of the 'third way' onto a more or less common denominator by way of a tolerant and solidaristic process of discussion. This is the elementary precondition for a position in economic policy that is both realistic and coherent, and here our specific tradition could enable us to make a decisive contribution, integrated into an overall project.

Clarification of the problem of the state and power would have a similar importance, in the present perspective of the contradictory struggle for influence on the state machine and for overcoming the spreading state-monopoly tendency in the direction of self-management based on grass-roots democracy.

Just as important, too, would be a comprehensive understanding of the path and goal of the cultural transformation which is the centrepiece of general human emancipation. This would mean paying extraordinary attention to the problems involved in the liquidation of patriarchy. The Green party can only be properly categorised and assessed against the background of the Green movement. It is the quite spontaneous attempt, an attempt thus undertaken with a certain necessity, to relate the new popular movement to the state and to national and international problems in general. Anyone who complains about the limitations of the average Green way of thinking, about how unpolitical the motivations of many of our allies are, should first understand the function of this emergence as a political party. It can become a most important learning process, and the situation in 1980 is well suited to accelerating this education. True, alongside the hasty formation of the new party with a view to the election campaign there is also a strengthened reproduction of conventional political bargaining and practices that are in no way alternative or grass-roots democratic. We should be self-critical enough to acknowledge our own share in this development. Nor should we overlook the fact that there are other important forces among the Green movement sensitive to these inadequacies; it is not only we who are unhappy with the traditional political forms. After the election we must play our part in examining in a spirit of solidarity where a virtue has all too quickly been made of necessity and where the movement has set up too much of an apparatus. Anyone who examines things more precisely should recognise that these non-alternative modes of behaviour are to be found right across the component traditions. In many respects the task for the Greens is to link up people from all 'camps' who think in a problem-oriented manner, and hence are open to change in themselves.

If this problem-oriented discussion and clarification gets under way, then the question as to whether and how 'the problems of the left can be overcome through the Green party' loses its significance. Where difference of cause, differences in approach, difficulties with terminology still prevail for a while, the principle of unity in diversity and diversity in unity gives us every possibility of emphasising our particular identity. Our perspective should be to become one of the currents that flow together in the movement, and though the sources are different, the waters will mix together as they move towards their goals, without any desire for a bland and distinction-free identity.

The Green party is by its very nature not an organisational challenge to us but an ideological challenge, and one that should be valued positively. It is not necessary for everyone to join it, important as it is that our forces are represented there adequately. More important is the spirit in which we collaborate, and this depends above all on how we assess the perspective. The ecology movement, which in its innermost core aims at human emancipation, must gain ground in all fields of our social and political life. It is an awakening that aims at saving our whole civilisation, and can only succeed if it reprogrammes the mode of production and way of life starting from the human individual.

From: Materialien zur ersten Sozialistischen Arbeitskonferenz
Spring 1980

What Are We Taking On? Thoughts on the Elements of a New Politics

No political tendency, however broad, is interesting chiefly for its own sake. The question is rather what relationship it has to the totality, what contribution it makes to the resultants of the historical process. If the following considerations relate particularly to the left, this is always with regard to the above stipulation. The internal constitution of the socialist forces in our country is unfortunately marked at the present time by the fact that it quite frequently disrupts collaboration with other progressive forces.

I am quite clear in my mind, moreover, that any 'we' that can realistically be discussed does not strictly exist as such. There is not a single left, there are simply leftists as a number of individuals who are for the most part isolated. I take this as an initial positive starting-point. After much — far too much — of what was hoped for since the 1960s has not come to pass, the organisational relics in which the former understanding of politics is perpetuated in fragmented form can only hinder us from liberating energies that have been wrongly tied up.

To this extent the title of the present essay should perhaps have run 'Quo vadis?' — what are *you* taking on, where are *you* going? But I believe the present situation is temporary, so I shall let the title stand. The answer must lie in personal responsibility, since at the present time there is no comprehensive and obligatory project to which everyone would owe allegiance and discipline. Solidarity is another question; but it can less than ever be demanded for particular standpoints.

With the Socialist Conference in Kassel we had our 'internal' social experiment. We can again relate to one another, to some extent even agree, if still more on form than on content. What was particularly important was that we also showed at least this much to those Social-Democrats who sought a dialogue with us because they are ultimately moved by the same problems as we are and thus have a positive interest in a left which is ready and willing for discussion outside its own party. And 'externally' we had the demonstration, also noticed by the media, that 'we are here'.

For all the inadequacy of preparatory information, practically everyone in the country who see themselves as on the left received the signal. As was subsequently said time and again, many more people still would have come if a signed invitation had appeared in the left press. Not all activists went into the various groupings after 1968-69. Others left these again in the course of time. And not least, in the 1970s, despite the decline of the movement, a portion of the next generation, as well as some older people too, newly developed a left sensibility, without joining an organisation and tying themselves to a too specific political conception. These forces, which quite evidently have a need for a cohesive orientation which will only come about through a process of collective self-understanding, can now come to the aid of those that had shut themselves away with fixed organisational and theoretical models.

It was precisely through the broadening of participation that the Kassel meeting pointed beyond the context of an inter-factional working conference. Although many lost causes still received spontaneous applause, most people who came were less interested in the assertion and comparison of positions than in new approaches to coming to grips with reality, no matter what position they were developed from. The influx of new forces without organisational ties contributes to the loosening of mental structures, to an opening towards reality. We must make still greater use of this at the next conference. The tendency to encapsulation and confinement to the conservation of forces which is bound up with the self-preservation interests of particular groups would only lead us still deeper into sterility, and then conferences would be of no use at all.

If in Kassel the windows were symbolically open, the next question will be what we want to call out of them, in such a way that it can be heard and taken up. What we have to say among ourselves is not enough, either in form or in content. Our political attitude only has a social significance if we do not cultivate it as an end in itself, if its effect goes beyond our reciprocal affirmation in one subculture among others. Certainly the 'left scene' has this social function, or more precisely, it *is* a social function. But to be on the left for and among other leftists ultimately doesn't get you anywhere, and thus leads so easily back into frustration, despite all the genuine or supposed correctness of penetrating analyses that are not intended for use outside a narrow circle.

If we are not prepared to deal with and relate to wider forces than our own, our controversy about ecology will remain inconsequential and academic. The challenge of the ecology crisis, and above all its articulation by a genuine mass movement, would not be faced by our discussion. And the reason for this does not lie in the positions in dispute, but rather in the introverted system of reference of the dialogue itself. Whether made explicit or not, certain 'basic truths' are assumed and arguments measured against them. This leads to the atmosphere of a party meeting, where the assertion that someone or something is not Marxist is already taken as a valid judgement as to the content involved. In this way we automatically close ourselves off from other forces who would be willing to discuss problems with us, but not 'on a principled basis'. People who are involved in other contexts of work and institution will only be attracted to participate with us if they see a possibility of contributing to the formation of opinion. Before the conference I wrote letters to Erhard Eppler,[26] Herbert Gruhl and Ivan Illich. If they had come, would they have found an atmosphere of readiness to hear what they had to say, for without this their appearance would have had no sense? Or would we still know everything better?

In today's conditions we shall not only proceed in the most rational way, but also the most expedient, if we take off our glasses and direct our thinking to reality unperturbed by a set of concepts prescribed in advance. It was no other than Engels who advised us: 'Marxism is not a dogma, but a guide to action'. The conceptual framework we have been accustomed to use relates to a different state of the world, both in form and in content. In the world of today it is only natural that it grasps those aspects which still correspond to the old situation. And undoubtedly there is a continuity. But precisely what is new, which is what really counts, then easily remains outside the field of view, or does not appear in its real importance. Some elements may remain, yet the situation alter completely if new elements appear, if everything changes in relation to everything else and the dominant aspect accordingly shifts. What good is it keeping verbal positions which enable you to criticise things in a defensive way, but not to change them? The legacy is only alive in so far as we invest it in a dynamic project. We shall make progress if instead of comparing our positions with one another and with the original texts, we add to the project and improve it in a reciprocal manner.

What Could Be the Starting-Point of Such a Project?

The very point we choose for our entry could have its implications, and in certain circumstances unthought-out ones. The theme of the 'ruling bloc' suggests a way of immediately getting to the political level. Instead of this, in considering our project we should directly get down to the *foundation* of the social totality. If we too directly rush in to discuss the power system, its internal differentiation, our conduct towards the state, the institutions, the various parties, and particularly the Social-Democrats, we can easily overlook how deeply the relative stability of political conditions is rooted in combinations of social interest. The ruling bloc is undoubtedly an expression of the given mode of production and way of life in general.

If the political-ideological formations (the 'blocs' — I ignore for the time the question of whether we might perhaps find a better expression for them) are delineated in terms of their attitudes for or against basic changes in the total system, the same is not true of the institutions of society (state, parties, associations, etc., including their apparatuses), taken in and for themselves. Of course these apparatuses are by nature conservative in terms of their structure, but the goals of their operation are not unchangeable. In this respect I probably formulated things in too absolute terms when I indiscriminately classed the SPD in its capacity as a party of government as belonging to the forces of inertia.[27]

Marxism has always emphasised the dual character of leadership functions, of social authority in general, and differentiated between domination over people and the administration of things, much as the two are linked together in the practice of class societies. It seems an attempt devoid of prospects, however, to seek to cast off the domination aspect of the state functions (which moreover cannot just be reduced to repression — a reductionist concept of the state such as this is unfruitful) with a single revolutionary shrug of the social shoulders. Indeed, we can only conceive of overcoming statism through a *long-run* process of *supersession,* i.e. above all its subordination to the control of the forces at the social base.

But if this is the case, we must necessarily treat the state machine as an *ambivalent* tool. In the new situation this is forced on us quite empirically: we have no other choice. It is absolutely improbable that the rapid and far-reaching process of social learning that alone can facilitate the transformation in civilisation will take place in good time if it is only propelled by the so-called forces of protest and is supposed to take place in confrontation with the official institutions, means of mass communication, etc. Nothing would then be more probable than the mutual obstruction of forces while the train goes ahead in the old direction. Society must transform its present apparatus into the instrument of reorganisation, on pain of its own destruction. *How* this is to be achieved, *how* the different special interests that now compete to subordinate this apparatus and that often simply paralyse it can be pressed back and subjugated, is one of the most important problems of our future.

Still more important, however, I see the decision whether we are to view things in a national or a global context, i.e. whether we intend to 'introduce' first the European and then the international aspect, or immediately think 'from the margins'. In both cases the same realities would come into view, but in very different perspectives. Immediate application to the domestic political situation with the many imponderables of its national history bears a grave danger of provincialism, and — in our particular case — also of underestimating our forces, which are from the start part of a more comprehensive potential.

Industrial Civilisation and the Crisis of Humanity

The idea that it is external contradictions that dominate today, for every country and even every region, is based on the fact that the capitalist economy presents a total world system, a totality that embraces all aspects. This not only includes the First and Third Worlds, the Second World of the Eastern bloc is also being gradually articulated into the general world market. And if the reproach once made by the Chinese that the Soviet Union was following the capitalist road is wrong as far as the nature of the *relations* of production there is concerned, it is all the more true as regards the production machine with which Soviet society is operating, and the corresponding form of demand for material goods. Not only the Russian revolution, but also the Chinese — it is now to be feared — have been unable to break with the horizon of capitalist civilisation. This is why the most general denominator of those external contradictions that overshadow the dynamic of internal class struggle in the developed capitalist countries is the drama between the capitalist metropolis(es) and the periphery.

The Russian revolution was the first response of what was originally a non-capitalist periphery to the global colonialism of 'Western' civilisation. It was the first anti-imperialist and anti-colonial revolution. This is the basis of its world-historic importance, which is now being ever more contradicted by the role of the Soviet Union as second superpower. The bloc confrontation between East and West inscribes the result of the first great collision between metropolis and periphery in such a way that the dynamic of this conflict has come to focus ominously on the arms race.

Caught up in a global strategic competition with the capitalist centre, which continues to lay down the rules, the Soviet Union is coming into ever more fundamental opposition to the peoples and states of the Third World. In its present constitution it does not present, nor does the Eastern bloc as a whole, any factor from which the progressive forces in the rest of the world could draw succour and relate to in a positive way — with any kind of solidarity, however critical. We can only take the Eastern bloc into account as a power factor, and analyse the interests that lie behind its policies. For this we need to consider in greater detail possible contents and forms of direct and indirect cooperation with the opposition forces on the other side of the bloc division, keeping in mind their whole scope, which reaches right into the ruling parties. The domestic balance of forces must shift on both sides. In this connection it still remains important to maintain a practical distance from the forces of the Cold War and to develop initiatives which go beyond the policy of détente and are oriented towards a bloc-free and alliance-free Germany and Europe.

In order to give resistance to the military madness a form that speaks to people as an individual duty, certain Christians have begun to collect signatures to the following declaration: 'I am prepared to live without the protection of armaments. I intend to work in our state for peace to be developed politically without weapons.' Couldn't a grass-roots mobilisation along these lines give the struggle for disarmament a new dimension?

The situation in the metropolises also determines the quest for a domestic political alternative to the practice of the dominant bloc. The lower classes, in fact all of us in the 'central' countries, profit on a large scale from the exploitation of labour-power and even more so from the plundering of resources from all the less developed countries of the world. They share an objective interest in the mass of profit extracted, in the continuity of supplies of raw materials at the lowest possible prices, in the defence of the privileged world-market position of their own society. The gulf that has opened in the North-South direction, and is increasing in depth every year, can foster the cohesion of the rich nations under the ideological hegemony of the dominant forces. Our experience with the problem of 'guest workers' already points in this direction.

It has become indisputably clear in the meantime that the gap between North and South cannot be narrowed by any kind of 'development aid' in the context of the capitalist world economy, whether this is 0.3 per cent or 0.7 per cent of gross national product. The reality is that every advance made in the kind of standard of living we enjoy here drives humanity as a whole deeper into its contradictions and makes these still harder to resolve. As long as we do not appreciate this basic failure of solidarity, we are only shedding crocodile tears when we talk about how we want to oppose our involvement in colonialism.

It is the model of our civilisation as a whole that most decisively bars the way to the rest of humanity. Let us imagine what it would mean if the raw material and energy consumption of our society were extended to the 4.5 billion people living today, or to the 10-15 billion there will probably be tomorrow. It is readily apparent that the planet can only support such volumes of production and their implications for the environment for a short time to come. On the other hand, the peoples of the Third World are being continually exposed to the standard set by our civilisation. Can we maintain this civilisation in its existing form while we know that humanity as a whole will have difficulty in living according to such a pattern? And while we can only hope that it will not even attempt to do so?

The type of industrial civilisation that has spread out from Europe is leading the whole of humanity into an inescapable dilemma. We know that the number of people that can be fed and provided for on a certain territory depends on their mode of production. For example, all calculations according to which the earth could supply bread for an ever growing world population assume an agriculture that is pursued industrially and supported by the massive application of fertilisers. Apart from the destruction of the soil's fertility that threatens even in the medium term, these fertilisers are also finite resources. If the whole enterprise of expanding industrial production is continued as long as it is still possible, with ever greater consumption of ever weaker concentrations of raw materials, we shall be faced at the end of the day with a production machine that is grinding to a halt for want of supplies of materials, yet without whose operation the given population cannot be maintained.

A resolution of the North-South conflict in the spirit of solidarity requires as an indispensable condition that our production machine here is no longer expanded, but rather diminished, that it is reconstructed and reprogrammed so that the sum of things which everyone needs to have no longer grows beyond the limits drawn by the finite extent of the earth. We must therefore determine afresh our material *demand* — starting from the basic *needs* of the human species as quite reliably ascertained by anthropology, and from the goal of production as the most complete development possible for all individuals. For this we require first of all a debate that embraces the whole of society, with the aid of the means of mass communication, which in this case would have to operate according to their concept (communication of the masses). The point is to agree on a social order in which production oriented to need is possible.

Political culture will only survive if a broad agreement as to how we want to change can be arrived at in good time. If things come to a terrible end in the form of wars of redivision and civil wars, forced rationing and eco-fascism, this will not be primarily because there are interested parties and ideologists who actively support these alternatives. In the decade now beginning the battles over distribution in the metropolitan countries will quite probably intensify. But if this is all, then the totality will simply continue on the old lines, according to the motto: justice (our little justice) must be done, even if the world perishes. It has been decisively pointed out, by André Gorz among others, that this policy simply helps to reproduce social injustice, so that the result is merely the 'modernisation of poverty'.[28]

This does not mean that the many internal social contradictions no longer play a role, but rather that they have a subordinate importance in a wider context, and thus obtain a different significance. They must above all be handled in such a way that they do not intensify the international contradictions. The domestic goal must be to live better with a reduced production (in terms of material quantity), i.e. with less labour and equalised incomes.

Footholds for a Strategy of Transformation

At the theoretical level, we must examine the entire coordinate system of our goals. General emancipation will be based on a quite different economic system from the one we used to imagine. If we do not heed the warning now, if we fail to understand, as Pharaoh did, the dream of the seven fat cows and the seven lean cows, then we shall certainly not have any general emancipation — or only after a new advance by those who remain after the last dance which ends our present great feast. A contraction in per capita output will inevitably follow from the shortage of resources and the requirements of an ecologically balanced economy.

Against the background of the North-South conflict and the situation in the metropolises, it is quite clear that it is simply impossible to base an overall strategy on the *immediate* economic interests of the 'Western' or 'Northern' working classes — no matter how we may define these. For this would mean taking our stand firmly on the basis of the metropolitan social partnership, i.e. of colonialism, as the trade unions do in so far as they express the alliance in growth of capital and labour: an orientation to the competitiveness of one's own country and one's own branch of industry, one's own corporation, one's own factory as the common goal. For our part, we can never achieve a real independence from such positions if our main object is to express these immediate interests even better. Certain comrades take a position that is anything but radical if they keep repeating in *this* debate that in our own country there are people who earn only 1500 marks per month (in which case they should have a lot more to say about the unemployed and other marginalised groups), and ask what they are supposed to 'give up'. At the rational level this argument shows a complete lack of understanding, and at the emotional level a flight from reality which seems quite deliberate. Poverty in the metropolises can always be appealed to in order to obstruct the development of genuinely radical opposition standpoints, for as long as capitalist conditions are reproduced.

The question then is not to ignore these immediate and short-run interests which by their very nature are chained to the system, because, as someone recently joked, they 'don't suit the purpose of world history'.

These interests precisely absorb the quantity of available mental energy that is needed to change the world. Within the metropolises, a front *against* these interests (as is unavoidably developing outside the metropolises) would be a strategy devoid of prospects, a false front that would only aggravate the situation (viz. the Red Army Fraction and its periphery: terror is not radical, it is not radical to provoke fear in the majority).

What is really radical is to think from the standpoint of the interests of humanity as a whole, and to resolutely articulate from this standpoint the long-run interests of one's own population. The SDP and the trade unions have an effective monopoly in representing the political and economic interests of the wage-earners, and there are genuine socialists in these organisations as well as others who may become socialists. These forces must be motivated to work with us in order to break the domination of the reform potential by a gradualism devoid of perspective, and to transform the balance of forces within these organisations themselves. Socialists both outside and within the SPD may continue to assert that the party is ultimately unchangeable, but 'While there's life, there's hope.'

A fruitful collaboration across party lines — and the ideological process can achieve this by its very nature — presupposes first of all that we learn to distinguish quite clearly between our assessment of the SPD and the trade unions as institutions largely tied into the ruling bloc, and our attitude towards individuals belonging to them.

Secondly, it presupposes that we at least concede the possibility that within these organisations long-run interests may prevail over short-run, general interests over particular. It is necessary to admit this hypothesis if only because the existing grouping of political forces in this country, much as it is on the point of breaking down, can only change into a different pattern over the long term. Besides, this hypothesis must be conceded to those who (as yet) find the perspective of a general rearrangement of forces improbable. What may prove decisive is the spontaneous emergence of a consensus around a consistent orientation to international requirements and the long-run interests of the majority of our own population, since the continuation of things on their present lines is already disturbing very broad circles.

In the first place, experience is accumulating daily that the quality of life is no longer rising with industrial progress of the kind we have had up till now and with an increasing gross national product. On top of this, the permanent jeopardy in which the foundations of our life are placed by imperialist or imperial great-power and military policies, by the world-wide colonialism of the metropolises, by the syndrome of underdevelopment and the population explosion that is ultimately caused by this, by the global crisis of environment and resources, and by the tendency towards universal state-ification and bureaucratisation — all these are finding ever more frequent expression in effects that are directly experienced as a threat:

New nuclear missiles in our country; nuclear power stations and nuclear waste deposits on our doorstep; the sharpening of the international situation over oil supplies (which like the nuclear power stations is clearly bound up with the problem of energy); the pressure of immigration into the rich countries; the tearing up and concreting over of the countryside; the noise that is present on all sides; the denaturing and poisoning of water, air and foodstuffs; the invasion of privacy by data processing; and not least, the destruction of mental health as the outcome of the insecurity and isolation that are an inescapable result of the whole mode of production and way of life for people who grind against one another in hectic competition for a success and a consumption that are drained of meaning.

It really doesn't need any incitement, simply an oriented articulation of all these needs and an explanation of how their origin lies in the system. It is precisely here that the strategy of transformation in the developed countries must take hold, this is where the source of the so-called new social movements lies. The local action campaigns, alternative projects, ecology movement and women's movement signal that countless people who are not mobilised by specific economic class interests or political aspects in the narrower sense, or are no longer mobilised by these, proclaim and organise in diverse ways their resistance as individuals and personalities affected. This is why the different currents of this new social movement cannot be artificially separated. They merge at least partially into one another, since what they speak to in the individuals involved appears not in isolation, but in association. Often, the distinction is made only according to which motivation is decisive for the particular individual. The ecology movement seems to bring together the greatest number of motivations, adding them together and tending to integrate them. It is not by chance, therefore, that it comes to play a key role as a reference-point for all alternative elements of late-bourgeois society. Just as the immediate international threat to capitalism does not come from its metropolises, but rather from the margins, so at the national level it is affected not directly at its economic centre, in the exploitation of labour-power as the source of everything it has at its disposal, but rather concentrically 'from outside': the field on which the monopolistic dynamic of growth can develop is constricted by the conditions of capital realisation.

Some Pointers to New Fields of Conflict

In the last analysis it is a question of restricting the scale of _investments_ and controlling their execution and purpose so as to do justice to both nature and human beings. I am well aware of the theoretical incompleteness of the following remarks, which have simply an ad hoc character, a merely indicative function. The basic idea is that on top of the obstructions now inherent to the capitalist reproduction process, the most varied means of extra-economic pressure are needed so as to force the stream of economic life into a different direction, a stream which would like to continue flowing spontaneously in its former bed no matter how stony this is. If the stability of the system has up till now been dependent on economic growth, especially in West Germany, this must be reversed in such a way that the ecological context in the broadest sense becomes a condition of stability.

While we cannot see how big capital is to lose its power of disposal over all its present domains in a short space of time, it is possible at least to considerably restrict its effects, given sufficient social mobilisation against the consequences of its competitive expansion. What kind of processes are already having an objective effect in this direction? On the one hand, the peoples of the Third World are increasingly setting out to limit the supply of raw materials and energy. And prices will continue to rise. On the other hand, the trade unions will be forced in their wage bargaining to pursue a policy of systematic reduction in the supply of labour, i.e. the shortening of working hours in a whole range of ways, so as to prevent any kind of 'progress' that creates jobs detrimental to mental and physical well-being and having a deskilling rather than a developmental effect on people in the labour process.

Cooperative arrangements of production and living, which in many respects take care of their own supplies, similarly contribute towards a decrease in the amount of labour-power available, as well as a restriction in demand. The massive obstruction of industrial expansion plans (for example in the car industry), of nuclear and other power stations, motorways and airports under the pressure of local action groups would brake the expansion of whole branches of industry. On the consumption side, deliberately organised refusal to consume can spread against products of doubtful use-value or with a poor relationship between cost and benefit. Legislation is needed to impose on the economy rigorous tasks of cleaning up the natural environment and improving working conditions. State expenditure on the expansion of production, and the provision of credit for investments which have to create their own markets, must be combatted as sources of inflation, both within and outside of parliament. Last but not least, we should attack the strategic role of arms production. The combined effect of these tendencies would compel a new approach to the problem of employment, through the loss of jobs which is unavoidable given increasing labour productivity and declining output. The number of jobs as technical units could be divided among the people available for employment in such a way that full employment is ensured.

Just as in the struggle against armaments, we should not be misled in the struggle against economic expansion to seek an alibi in the 'enemy', i.e. in foreign competition, in the danger of a flight of capital abroad, etc. The same movement as is under way here will also develop and grow in the other metropolitan countries, and we must lend this our international solidarity. If it is happening first of all in the most industrialised and richest countries — such as Sweden, Holland, West Germany, Austria, Switzerland, even France — as shown by the relative strength of the ecology movement here, the new forces are intervening precisely at the right place. Where else should the spiral be halted if not here, where the pace and direction are set for the other European countries that still lag a little behind? Since an upward equalisation is impossible, there is no other way than to break off the pinnacle. 'Unilateral disarmament' in the production machine as well! The domestic social tensions that this brings with it must be endured and resolved, and in such a way that the burdens cannot be imposed on those at the bottom of society. Where is a policy of income equalisation possible, if not in a rich country such as this?

What is very important in this connection is that precisely those forces with the strongest interest in radical reforms, reforms with a revolutionary content, should understand the positive significance of the rule of law, not only defending the constitutional order against the attacks of reaction, but also paying attention to their own actions. Non-violent resistance such as that at the Gorleben power station site ultimately makes the other side impotent. Violence from our side only trains the repressive apparatus and isolates us. The alternative forces must strive to prevail in the balance of political-psychological forces. The greatest possible unity between end and means at every step will shorten our path in this direction. If there were a genuine ideological hegemony for change, then the repressive organs of the state could not be deployed against it. Moreover, the turn in civilisation that is necessary, the transformation of humanity's objective material culture and its subjective culture, is a task which violence can contribute nothing towards — except continued provocations which reveal how intolerable existing conditions are without pointing beyond them.

. . . And if We Take a New Path?

Whether the idea of the Socialist Conference has a future will depend on whether we manage to initiate projects in this direction (even in due course contributions to a *single* project: if this is not yet possible,it is at least necessary!), with a significance 'internally' for ourselves as well as 'externally'. This should take such a form that its fundamental contents correspond to and communicate with a wide basis of social interests. The constructive forces in our country, those who are seeking an alternative, genuinely need and expect something in this direction — even if they are still somewhat sceptical.

The first condition for a political project is certainly a realistic understanding of our own task and possibilities as the socialist left. By this I don't primarily mean an honest debate with the causes of our former weakness and fragmentation, necessary as this is. And I particularly don't hold the view that we should start by moderating our demands because we don't have the great opportunities open to the left in other West European countries, for the many objective and subjective reasons that are bound up with the Federal Republic of Germany as a special case. The 'German model' will very likely lose its allure in the 1980s, while it is precisely the relative economic and political stability in this most powerful European capitalist country that gives us an especially urgent responsibility, which undoubtedly has also an international dimension. In other words, I don't see it as though we have to lower our sights because we set them too high ten years ago. We should not rely on this psychological pendulum. What was wrong with our previous ideas was not their scope, but rather an inadequate idea of the process involved, of the result aimed at and of the source of energy for the whole undertaking, which must be a mass one.

At the Kassel conference we were united in acclaiming that we needed to find a new language in order to break out of our ghetto, but this is of course far more than just a question of pedagogy. The system of concepts we have used in the past, our traditional model of analysis and our socialist self-conception related to the working class have been rejected by reality. It is not that the descriptive and analytical achievements of Marx and his followers no longer have any relevance today. Most of these can still find confirmation in present conditions. But the paradigm as a whole has proved wrong, the conclusions derived from this approach are not on the horizon.

As long as we continue to perceive and address the actual working classes as if a proletariat with a world-historic mission was waiting in them for its time to arrive, as if their economic interests were accordingly the yardstick for social movements in general, we shall not get rid of our sectarian language, the sectarian character of our whole discourse. We are simply dealing with an object we have fashioned in our heads. If we cling to this way of thinking, then the interventions of our comrades from the Trotskyist League, for example, are no further removed from our own mental system than the caricature from the original; which is why we find it such a torture to listen to them. At Kassel I myself thought and spoke more conventionally than in other surroundings — and this was in no way a 'tactical calculation'. The closed society has a contaminating effect. Loyalty among comrades, which we need so much, easily slips into dealing with problems as they have been handed down — hence in a constrained and imprisoned fashion.

In formal terms we were agreed, with only few exceptions, that we have to bring ecology and economics together. What this meant in the first place of course was ecological and working-class interests. Yet ecology, this concept that originally denoted 'only' a discipline in natural science, refers in the present connection to human interests, and interests of humanity, that strike deep into the social space, and in this comprehensive sense it precedes and goes beyond economics.

Already on this point we were no longer in agreement. Some people said that what stirs people up against the world system of capital valorisation and the destruction of nature can still be integrated around the interests bound up with wage-labour. But they could not demonstrate how the contradiction between wage-labour and capital still operates as the centre and main source of mobilisation for a fundamental change in the world. Only then would the logical conclusion be the traditional one of a popular-front alliance with the working class as its core, and would it still be correct to give our publications names such as *Problems of Class Struggle* and *Workers' Fight*. Other interests would still have to be more or less subordinated.

The binding of our forces to an illusory perspective is all the more serious in its effects in so far as we really do find ourselves in a new situation, one that cannot be mastered by any particular 'class standpoint'. In the past the threat of a 'decline of the West' was the pessimistic perspective of terrified bourgeois who confused the general crisis of capitalism with the apocalypse of our civilisation itself. Today we must recognise that capitalism really can pull with it into the abyss the entire basis on which we are standing (and not only we 'Westerners'), unless there is a massive counter-movement against this.

If I get repeatedly drawn into what I see as an outdated debate on the concept of the proletariat, a debate which tends in my view to be right from the start a scholastic one, this is out of a desire that we might finally succeed in freeing ourselves from this earliest of our dogmas, and undertake our task in the field of the new social movements instead of becoming an obstacle in their way.

The Error in Banking on 'the' Proletariat

According to the classical idea of a workers' movement with a task for all
humanity, it goes without saying that this should take the defence of the
natural conditions of human existence as its cause, particularly when
these are now totally threatened by the same profit system that is its
traditional adversary. But the mere fact that the ecology crisis could
become a subject of *controversy*, and that an ecology movement has
grown up in the first place outside of the working class, shows that what
was a self-evident truth for 19th century Marxism is no longer so today.
The idea of a direct coincidence between (European) working-class
interests and those of the rest of humanity, the idea that it is enough to
refer to the 'class standpoint' in order to attain the level of a movement
for general emancipation, no longer applies. Marxism always assumed
that socialist theory had a function for society as a whole. But contrary to
expectations, this function will not succeed but is increasingly lost if it is
pursued by way of the particular interests of the Western working
classes, since in practice these prove not to coincide with general
interests. The organised workers' movement has not developed in the
direction anticipated, when taken as a whole and over the whole period of
time. The calculation contained in our concept of the proletariat has a
fundamental error, which we must ultimately settle accounts with.

Doesn't the whole troublesome business of class analysis show that the
class can no longer be conceived as a concretely acting unity, however
diligently people like to tot up strike figures? What exists, with various
differentiations, is the relationship of wage-dependence in the broadest
sense, and hence the corresponding structure of interests. This 'salariat',
however, as it is called in French, is essentially nothing more than the
conceptual summary for all those who among all their other interests as
social human beings also have a wage interest, quite independent of the
place and importance of this in their motivational hierarchy. In other
words, it is simply a logical category. Are the majority of those ascribed to
it moved *chiefly* by this interest? And what social role is played by that
section of the collective worker for which this interest does assume a key
value? What does it really mean, to juggle around with this one *aspect* of
material interests until a revolutionary potential is derived in a totally
abstract manner?

The fact that objective economic interests exist, arising from class
position, and that it is difficult to imagine someone for whom these have
no mental effect, says absolutely nothing about their historic potential. Is
it a question of a lack of consciousness (which simply needs to be brought
in from outside) if these interests do not dominate in the subjective
structure of interests? As a general rule people regularly direct their

mental energy to the real bottlenecks in their individual personal existence, and if their material reproduction seems to be more or less secured at a certain customary level they will only concentrate on it to the extent that this level appears directly endangered. This relief — however relative — is precisely one of the victories that the workers' movement in the highly industrialised countries has achieved. And for this very reason, the real problem now becomes how for the workers, too, the requirements of general emancipation can attain a decisive importance, even though class barriers still determine the specific conditions of struggle. The more developed the human personality, and the more it therefore lays claim to, the more people can seek to release energy from worries over the necessities of life and direct it into self-chosen, creative activities. It may well be that what is lacking above all are the forms of social organisation which these needs, often still only embryonic, require for their further development.

From Class Interests to Life Interests. Considerations on an Expanded Concept of Emancipation

In any case, *new* interests (material and ideal) of the *same* individuals are the focus of new social movements, which in fact point beyond the mere reproduction of the existing relations of production. One could of course decide to call *all* interests of people who in the narrower sense are wage-earning, i.e. workers, working-class interests, so that if someone takes a stand against nuclear power stations they do so *as* a worker. But there is no theoretical justification for this. If we previously asked which people's interests (the interests of which class) should historically prevail, we must now ask which human interests (which class of human interests) point towards a desirable future, and how these can be strengthened and effectively organised.

From a methodological standpoint, this means analysing the social structure at the level of psychological mediations (in both the social and individual sense), i.e. investigating in this way the specific structures of interest against which protest potentials are directed so that surplus energies can be concentrated on these. This means filling the psychological gap that has opened between economics and politics in standard Marxism. This will not hinder but rather help us in investigating the economic mechanisms, and above all the transforma-tions and final links by which the impulses that can be abstractly established within the economic machine determine social behaviour — in such a way, moreover, that the result is often reactions in conformity with the system, in one way or another. At all events, our effectiveness is suffering from the way that our traditional concept of class interests and thus of social interests in general is unpsychological and thus constantly seduces us into economistic reduction.

At the present time, it would mean thinking in precisely this false perspective if we expected the new mass movement to start legitimising itself according to the old criteria. It leads simply nowhere trying to calculate in advance the relative distance between the ecology movement and the trade unions. The problem is precisely that the threshold for a directly ecological or a general cultural-revolutionary commitment is higher in the mass organisations of the wage-earners, and this is so for understandable reasons. What is now called for is a most far-reaching opening towards the new requirements that is motivated by concern for the trade-union interests themselves, i.e. a revaluation of values within the organised working class itself, including for example the new focuses in wage bargaining that are ever more frequently desired by the rank and file.

If we proceed from the workers as people, there are objective contradictions *within* their disposition of interests, and these have to do with the relation between immediate and long-term requirements. In any case, there can be no doubt that the results of the ecology crisis, while they cannot in the main be directly applied in the confrontation between wage-labour and capital, will affect the workers at least as stubbornly as they do other social strata, especially in the future.

The question as to which elements of the social structure will ultimately provide the strongest impulse is a practical one, and cannot be decided by deduction from principles. But is it even the right question? Even where mass parties of the left are relatively open towards the alternative movements, we can see that these movements cannot be integrated around a class position as such, and this is so even though people who want to live differently are still subjected to the existing social structure and can to this extent be classified sociologically. What is most striking is their above-average level of education. It is this, and not the more or less well-established way they draw their incomes — not even the somewhat higher than average level of these incomes (which is often brought into debate) — that seems to me most significant, if we are concerned to assess perspectives for the future.

For educational level (and not only the formal level) is rising despite all reservations as to the 'material' and mental quality of the knowledge appropriated. The depth of the crisis of civilisation is shown precisely by the presence of this fundamental opposition from people who tend to be privileged both mentally and materially, yet who in large numbers are thinking of dropping out. We must investigate the real social interests of a *non-economic* kind that are seeking expression in this way. It could be interests in the development and growth of the personality, at least interests of identity, that form the underlying common denominator. Together with this, however, other criteria by which people want to change society also become important. Above all, people are injured chiefly in non-economic needs and by non-economic effects of the prevailing conditions, and hence react in certain circumstances more directly in this respect than in their economic interests. In order to find a strategy that affects the core of domination, and above all has a constructive effect for those participating in it, we must try to recognise the points at which there is closest connection between material (not only economic) interests and interests of the personality.

As I see it, therefore, the first question is to locate this shift in the centre of gravity of the structure of individual interests as a real tendency. I have still not tackled the question as to whether this is not too much to expect, given that the majority of people, and possibly even of young people, are still quite fundamentally trapped in the existing social relations. A long discussion would be needed to say all that could be said on this score. What concerns me first of all is to draw together those people who are already 'waiting for the call'. From all appearances — and I don't want to say any more at the moment — the organising factor which can bring the alternative forces together and give them a social coordination (as must be desired) will in future not be any particular class interest, but rather a long-term human interest. On the other hand, the social order facing dissolution will itself, *by its dysfunctioning,* focus the most varied forces against it — on the old fronts as well as the new.

At all events, it is important to bear in mind right from the start the great range of provocations with which the given system confronts the majority of the population. And we can do this without a preconceived certainty as to where the celebrated 'key link' lies. We have to participate in the attempt to bring together 'pluralistically' *all* those forces the system calls into action against itself at the most varied points, and to channel their energy into its natural direction against the cause of all evil in the driving mechanism of the capitalist system. It is likely that the cause itself will give rise to a new unifying tie that can hold together the parts.

Heretical Thoughts on the General Use of the Traditional Concept of the Proletariat

For all its dogmatic rigidities, the New Left with its origin in the student movement of the 1960s has a surreptitious affinity with the new social movements — because it was ultimately one of them itself and in a certain sense even their first wave, anticipating right at the start their fundamental theme, for example with respect to the Alternative movement. I am referring here simply to its original scope. Its fragmentation and ensuing narrowness resulted from the quest for a more substantial subject which could carry the various more or less revolutionary intentions towards their goal. What has now become still clearer to me than in my first weeks and months in West Germany is that the identification with the working class — in the wake of so many generations of intellectuals who sought their army here when there was still a prospect of finding such a force — was a mental regression from a completely new perspective that was scarcely prefigured in previous history and was not to be mastered overnight.

The May events in Paris objectively pointed forward in a quite new direction. Those who still speak about the 'betrayal of the French Communist Party' at that time (the Trotskyist comrades with their classical Marxism, essentially a form of Leninism), being set on finally establishing the correct party, probably bear a greater responsibility for this regression on the part of the revolutionary youth than a latecomer such as myself could initially recognise. Since then, I have heard too many comrades from *several* of the subsequent splinter groups and parties tell how they went through the Fourth International at one point or other. This would not be the first time, at any rate, that a vanguard disguises itself in the cast-off clothing of an earlier and unfinished revolution.

One thing, however, the quest for the revolutionary subject made completely clear: the New Left — taken for itself, outside the main field of the new movement that was still impending — was a phenomenon of the intellectuals. There is no reason to deny this or be ashamed of it; we should be openly aware of the very wide range of implications that this has. Perhaps the most important of these is that it cannot produce the totality from itself, it is not in itself sufficient. Schiller's motto then applies: 'Always strive for the whole. And if you cannot become a whole yourself, join up with a whole as a serving member.'[29] We must try to formulate our project not in terms of our experimental identities, but rather proceeding from the new realities and in view of the actual forces and interests which we wish to serve. To relate this once again to the present 'appeal': for Marx, the transition to the working-class standpoint was based on the clear assumption that this was the necessary mediation towards a practice of transformation *for the totality*. If this condition has altered, that does not mean an end to the task of advancing to an understanding of the overall historic movement in the service of society. But then this movement must be differently mediated, by a different subject, and this subject need not necessarily be a particular economic class. History knows other combinations, and at the present time a new combination is emerging.

It is precisely if we remain tied to the concept of the proletariat that we lose our socialist perspective. According to our definition, the proletariat was not a class of bourgeois society, i.e. the workers in their capacity as a class pointed beyond the capitalist horizon. The proletariat was defined in such a way that it could carry the ideal of general human emancipation. In this connection, the mechanism of mobilisation for this world-historic role was conceived in effectively economic terms; the antagonistic conflict of interests over the conditions for the sale of labour-power was supposed to provide the energy to shatter the old social framework. What has happened instead is that the capital relationship and with it bourgeois society is reproduced relatively smoothly in this basic contradiction, and the movements that point beyond the context of the capitalist system are visibly developing not in terms of this general class position but rather around other, more specific stimuli, in which people are affected less in terms of their class membership than as concrete individuals.

The Revolt of Individuality

If we assume that late capitalism both produces and frustrates more *individuality* than any former mode of production, one problem which then arises is that the subjective forces have scarcely any chance of becoming appropriately effective in a distribution struggle which has become an institutionalised ritual. Commitment to humanity only means something positive either when space is defended for the preservation and development of individuality, or when attempts are made at a new cultural framework, a new way of working and living. And are these not much rather the ways leading beyond the existing state of affairs, whereas in the traditional economic conflicts people are perpetually swung on the roundabout kept in motion by the driving mechanism of capitalist competition?

The real damage of maintaining a 'class orientation' consists ultimately in diverting attention from a recognition and dynamisation of the actual forces of resistance in the individual. What strikes us as the 'new social movements', and politically as a kind of 'revolt of the centre', is the erupting revolt of individuality along a number of different lines against the end-products of the capitalist system. This is where the common denominator lies. The antithesis which these all seek is 'a different life', a completely different civilisation. The ecology crisis and its absolute pinnacle, the danger of total annihilation in the short term by nuclear war, provide the fundamental challenge from which the mobilisation of energy proceeds.

Those of us who are presently working in one way or another with the

Green, Multicoloured and Alternative movements have by this very token taken a leap forward in effectiveness and the ability to communicate, and for all the difficulties and contradictions we have also attained a more optimistic perspective. Our function for this new mass movement reminds us that the socialist left is a necessary organ which society requires in order to change itself. It is certainly no accident that analogous forces in other European countries — the Socialist Left Party in Norway, the Left Party (Communist) in Sweden, the Progressive Organisations now gaining ground in Switzerland and the French PSU — have all turned towards ecology, and to a greater or lesser extent towards the other new social movements such as the women's movement as well. The same orientation is gradually gaining ground in the large Eurocommunist parties as well as among the youth sections of the Social-Democrats. It is in fact becoming more and more likely that the hopes for emancipation will focus precisely around these new movements. They cannot expect any help with their projects from the established parties, including the Social-Democrats, only all kinds of manoeuvres designed to capture and contain them. The objective task is therefore to transform our theoretical knowledge and our social experience into a dynamic project of comprehensive societal scope, which genuinely does integrate what is present at the level of interests. Whether we are able to do so will also depend on how we concretely involve ourselves.

It goes without saying that our own interests as intellectuals affected by the present situation (as men, and particularly as women) will also play a role in our projects. As intellectuals, however, who have committed ourselves to general interests out of a 'rational egoism', and more or less adopted these general interests as our own. At all events, our chief task lies in the attempt, which of course cannot be free of ideology, to express what kinds of change society as a whole needs. And in this connection we proceed from the way we are ourselves generally affected, at clear moments even with an awareness of our own particular interest.

In the last analysis it lies in the nature of things that people whose main concerns are of this kind should normally orient themselves to the 'left', i.e. to social changes that above all improve the opportunities of human advance for those who are at present hard done by, precisely because, as Marx and Engels put it in the *Communist Manifesto*, 'the free development of each is the condition for the free development of all'. We must produce a consensus for appropriate alternatives, against the other consensus which the ruling bloc, supported by the 'normative power of established fact' and by its dominance in the mass media, is still able to impose on the majority. In the struggle to express long-term interests and their mediation with the short-term, what matters is the starting-point in the individual, where emancipatory and survival interests lie so close alongside that the spark can spread from one to the other.

Besides, there is more surplus consciousness around now than at any previous time of crisis in history, and in so far as we understand that we are ourselves the organ of this, we can move in a homogenous material — if it turns out that the emancipatory interests of individuals tend to point in the same direction. People's material interests may differ, as these are ordered by their position in the social structure. Ever more frequently, however, these interests are consciously subordinated to the goal of achieving the parameters of an existence oriented towards self-affirmation and self-realisation. The elaboration of one's individuality, not the accumulation of material values but the securing of the conditions of work and development, directly becomes the motive force and regulator of economic action as well.

Today this motivation is coming to the fore in *all* strata of the collective worker; the most energetic people, and those strongest in their mental demands, are at some point or other undertaking the attempt to begin a creative life for themselves even if this means a reduction in their living standard and external security. Isn't this also the specific impulse behind the women's movement? Can its goals be reached without a different kind of everyday life, a different structure of needs, a different technology and organisation of production, without completely different standards of human achievement and human value?

In the last analysis, the emancipatory interests not only have a greater potential than ever before, because a greater quantity of mental energy is finding expression in them, but on top of this we are also pursued by a more powerful pressure of danger than ever before. While the magnitude of the emancipatory potential depends on how much surplus consciousness is liberated from the prevailing models of need satisfaction, its intensity is determined by the challenges to which it reacts. In such situations, people's long-run interests as human beings can tend to prevail over their immediate economic interests even in the privileged classes, so that it becomes possible to formulate these long-run interests and give expression to them across class divisions. In times of a general crisis of civilisation, this has always been the function of the progressive intelligentsia: inthe face of a society stuck fast in its institutions, to point the way forward that leads beyond the *total* matrix. Here it is apparent that the ecological position is also the radical socialist one. To sketch out a project for this, a counter-project to the blind calculation that prevails in the system of power, is equally in the general interest and in our own particular interest, i.e. it is also our own most basic concern. It can only arise if people who are ready for a new departure come together from all the major traditional camps, if they consciously work on one another and seek allies even at the heart of the institutional system.

Instead of our own party, which some of us would still like, we should create an 'ideologically neutral' forum where *everyone* who wants to take part in political planning oriented to concrete problems can meet together. Labels have become completely treacherous. Even the label 'left' is no longer automatically progressive. It should not matter at all that some people class themselves as conservative Greens or right-wing Social-Democrats — not to mention the large field in between — as long as they want to play a productive part in the discussion about fundamental changes. From left-wing and ecologically committed Social-Democrats, in particular, we have had writings which are far richer and more precise in content, and give a more realistic impression (at least on first reading), than most of what is produced to the left of the SPD and even in the Green party. It would be irresponsible to try and ignore these forces. We should most definitely conduct our undertaking in such a way that these people feel invited to join in. Naturally, genuine liberals are included as well, and we should even open ourselves to the left wing of the Christian-Democrats. Work must be conducted in such a fashion that our allies take part primarily as individuals — not denying their political identities, but not as representatives of their parties and groups.

This would of course require a preparation that goes beyond our own circles, and above all a careful definition of the subjects for discussion. We can perhaps find a different name, which sums up the broad spectrum better than the description 'Socialist Conference', for example 'Third Way Forum'. This concept is suitable precisely because of its openness towards the most diverse contents, which however are all linked with the intention of rising above the dilemma of the two 'world systems'. It will also be used by forces who still remain within the established parties. Some people will conclude from this that it is inappropriate. My own conclusion is the opposite. I see the use of this concept as indicating a recognisable desire to attain the party of ecological reason and real humanism. The way leading out of the present situation need not be conceived of as 'socialism' by all who want to tread it. There are indeed people who have turned away from this precisely in the name of the emancipatory hopes attached to the concept of socialism, since they have seen their ideal perverted under this name. All that matters is the direction in which the various efforts converge.

This could lead to a centre of attraction for the most varied constructive forces interested in a non-party or supra-party discussion. The precondition on our side would be to set aside our special identity and place it in the service of a more comprehensive cause, affirming it only in grappling with concrete problems, rather than in the assertion of a priori positions. This is precisely something that our non-aligned forces can be good for, and in this way we could rise above our position as the left, i.e. above the barriers that lie in our former ideology and practice. We need the opportunity to change ourselves, and this lies in an advance into the midst of society, into the midst of its problems.

Summer 1980

Conditions for a Socialist Perspective in the Late Twentieth Century

Dear comrades,

It is naturally my own experiences of 'actually existing socialism', which I have sought to explain as a path of independent development on a non-capitalist road, that form the background to what I want to say today. But I did not originally intend, when I left the GDR, to play the role of an East European dissident in the West, a role that is easy to get into if you are classified as a specialist in Eastern bloc affairs. I wanted to change countries, but not fronts, and so the most important thing for me first of all was to understand as much as possible about the changes that are due in the metropolitan countries.

This was all the more necessary, given that the whole history of the Soviet Union since 1917, and of Eastern Europe since 1945, remains incomprehensible without the pressing challenge posed *from outside*. Modernise, industrialise, make wooden Russia into iron Russia, the imperative to 'catch up and overtake' — that is the basic text of this history. And if this made it possible to avoid direct dependence, it certainly did not avoid indirect dependence. Since the start of the colonial era, we cannot correctly analyse and historically assess any event or even any atrocity in any country of the 'Eastern' Second World or 'Southern' Third World without first asking whether the ultimate cause is not to be sought in the First World, in the last instance in the accumulation of capital and development of the world market that spreads out from here. Of course, the relationship of metropolis and periphery has been reciprocal from the beginning, but under the dominance of the metropolitan economy.

For this reason, I did not act as an émigré after I was relieved of GDR citizenship, nor as a 'regime critic' as the bourgeois media in West Germany put it, but immediately involved myself in a new political practice. The theme of this new practice is one which today in the West increasingly provides the key to an effective politics for the left: the connection between ecology and socialism, a new definition of the socialist perspective in view of the global ecological crisis with which the capitalist industrial system is now threatening a total catastrophe for humanity.

This ecological crisis is not the subject of my present talk, but it is the driving motive of my concern for a truly contemporary concept of socialism. For this reason I would like briefly to forestall the misunderstanding that the point at issue is principally one of environmental pollution, which in fact provides only *one* subordinate aspect. Its importance, taken in isolation, is chiefly that it offers a *direct* point to link up with in the metropolitan countries, motivating people to resistance in a radical way that is no longer generated by the traditional class struggle over income distribution.

The true dimension of the ecology crisis has been recently summed up by the British historian Edward Thompson, prominent in the new peace movement. He has coined the term 'exterminism' for the tendency to the self-extinction of the human race that is present in the growing independence of the arms race from even the rational interests of its most powerful protagonists.[30]

But this exterminism is in no way confined to the danger of nuclear war. It is equally to be found in the absolute impoverishment to which the capitalist model of growth condemns half humanity. The metropolitan industrial system, with its branches on every continent, is already the reason why a tenth of the world population is exposed to the extreme physical degradation of starvation, while a further third is pressed below the subsistence level.

Not least, and inseparably connected with the military and economic aggression, exterminism is expressed in the destruction of the natural basis of our existence as a species. In the metropolises themselves, this can for a time still be dealt with by an expensive work of repair — though a profitable one, so far as private capital is involved in it. On the periphery, however, and in the so-called threshold countries, the consequences are irreparable, and ultimately react on humanity as a whole. The result of our efforts is the destruction of whole species of plants and animals. By cutting down forests, we interrupt the production of the very oxygen that we breathe, while our industry also burns up more and more. We poison the atmosphere, heating it up until self-regulation of the climate is destroyed not just locally, but on a world scale. We let loose millions of chemicals on human beings, plants, land and sea, without even being able to assess the consequences for each individual case or for the short term.

This is an overall crisis of our civilisation, which is backfiring on human nature. Scarcely has the earlier kind of material want been more or less banished from the metropolises, before people are plagued by cancer and crime, heart-attacks and mental illness. The destruction of nature by industrial accumulation, the danger of nuclear war, the impoverishment of marginalised masses in the Third World, mental impoverishment in the metropolises — these are the horsemen of the apocalypse at the end of the second Christian millenium. And apart from the fact that repression of all kinds is the response to any attempt to offer them some resistance, we have not yet focussed our powers of understanding sufficiently to look them in the face, to make out the essence and source of their countless manifestations.

In the last analysis, we are faced with a new dimension of the alternative 'socialism or barbarism', one that was originally unsuspected. We find ourselves forced to conceive of socialism differently from Marx on one point above all. For him, socialism was a classless industrial society; and the industrial aspect of this was to be more or less unproblematically the legacy of capitalism. Marx and Engels went so far as to write in the *Communist Manifesto:*[31]

> The bourgeoisie has through its exploitation of the world market given a cosmopolitan character to production and consumption in every country. To the great chagrin of reactionists, it has drawn from under the feet of industry the national ground on which it stood. All old-established national industries have been destroyed or are daily being destroyed. They are dislodged by new industries, whose introduction becomes a life and death question for all civilised nations, by industries that no longer work up indigenous raw material, but raw material drawn from the remotest zones; industries whose products are consumed, not only at home, but in every quarter of the globe. In place of the old wants, satisfied by the productions of the country, we find new wants, requiring for their satisfaction the products of distant lands and climes. In place of the old local and national seclusion and self-sufficiency, we have intercourse in every direction, universal interdependence of nations ...
>
> The bourgeoisie, by the rapid improvement of all instruments of production, by the immensely facilitated means of communication, draws all, even the most barbarian, nations into civilisation. The cheap prices of its commodities are the heavy artillery with which it batters down all Chinese walls, with which it forces the barbarians' intensely obstinate hatred of foreigners to capitulate.

We can no longer share the spirit in which this was written.

Anyone who has lived in Eastern Europe has an experience that goes beyond all theory: industrialism, productivism, Fordism, etc. obstruct the socialist exit rather than lead to it. And the suspicion has arisen in the meantime that not only does this happen with an industrialisation that is directly dependent, or — as in the Eastern bloc — indirectly dependent, but it happens with every known kind of industrialisation, so that the means generally gobbles up the end, which was to have been freedom, love, happiness for all.

When I wrote the conclusion to my book *The Alternative* I already suspected that we need to criticise not only the capitalist aspect of industry and accumulation, but also accumulation itself; not only the economic form, but the material content of industrial civilisation. And the reason for this is that it seems simply impossible to make in reality the division that is so easy in theory between science and technique on the one hand and their capitalist application on the other.

I certainly still believe that the Russian revolution had no real alternative to an industrialisation designed to catch up with the West, no alternative therefore to political despotism. But I am in the process of revising the view still put forward in the first two parts of *The Alternative,* the analytic parts, that all countries have to pass through the crucible of industrialisation, that socialism always presupposes mature industrialism, and that it does so in the sense that is predefined by the level so far reached in the metropolises, predefining therefore the *manner in which* human beings must satisfy their needs.

I was still trapped by the experience of the Soviet road, and — as I now see it — by its first, purely immanent negation by Trotskyism, which has still not understood that while Stalinism was an excessive Leninism that was unforeseen, it was still Leninism for all that. When I wrote *The Alternative,* it was not yet clear to me that the positions from which we can deduce not only a theoretical and ideological counter-model to the Soviet one, but at least the beginnings of a practical counter-model too, are far more to be sought in Kronstadt than among the victors over Kronstadt, and far more in Bukharin, the so-called rightist, who wanted to leave the peasants a certain space for autonomous development, than in the so-called left industrialisers (. . .)

After these preliminary remarks, then, on to my proper subject. What can be meant by 'new socialism'? What is new, it seems to me, will lie more in the changed conditions, and less in the model of socialism itself, i.e. less in the concrete utopia we want to pursue. I naturally see it as important to purge our concept of the goal from illusions of progress of an industrialist and techno-bureaucratic kind. But beyond this corrective we shall scarcely come up against any elements that have not already emerged in the writings of one or other of the old socialists, including of course the utopians. Moreover, I also include here the anarchist legacy, especially its orientation to communities accessible to communicative and cooperative self-management. What particularly remains unchanged is the goal of general human emancipation, i.e. of a society that is in every respect classless, basically conceived around a notion of the human being, the ideal of free individuality in all-round development.

Leaving aside formulations determined by their particular time, this must refer to a certain constant, an *anthropological* constant. Communism is not to be an arbitrary construction, but precisely the order suited to fully developed human nature. This pre-historic constant, however, and its position in the general context of nature, must be given a fresh polish in our theory today. We can see in the industrially developed countries how the per capita consumption of materials and energy can rise to infinity without this indicating a leap into the realm of freedom for the consuming individuals, while it is rather Huxley's *Brave New World* or Orwell's *1984* that present the models of the most productivist society. Independent of the historical form of their satisfaction, then, which may well not be long sustainable, what are the basic needs of the human being as a social creature, i.e. once physical reproduction has been secured?

If we ask this question, we come up against needs such as that for social security, which can ultimately be satisfied only by the safety of a community. Then there is the need arising from this for developmental stimuli of a quality that can lead to the ability to appropriate the culture of the time. This assumes personal communication that can support confidence and hope. Then the need for recognition by others of the individuality that arises in this way. And ultimately the need for self-realisation and growth as a personality.

These needs are certainly 'non-material', at least in the bodily sense; to use a somewhat old-fashioned expression, they are needs of heart and spirit, which together used to be called the soul, their ultimate link being the desire to love and be loved. We must recognise this and understand it right through to the inclination to spiritual transcendence, as the irreplaceable source from which revolution can draw its decisive power to prevail, and always has done where it has been victorious.

I am convinced that the socialist idea only becomes radical by pointing beyond the struggle to secure the means of subsistence, in the direction I have indicated. Otherwise it happens time and again, precisely in the event of our victory, that we oppose bread and freedom to one another, as in Dostoyevsky's celebrated legend of the Grand Inquisitor, that for the sake of material provision we are content to leave those who are provided for in their subaltern state. In the dependently industrialising countries today, we have a situation where the material minimum can only be extracted, i.e. where marginalisation can only be overcome, by those affected raising themselves to political self-consciousness, to the full claim to human dignity, to the free development of each individual.

Let me try to understand the situation in Venezuela. A parasitic bourgeoisie, half state half private, which with 5 per cent of the population grabs more than half the national income. A middle class of around a third of the population, whose existence is largely bound up with the country's landowner status, i.e. with their share in the revenue from oil received by the state class and speculators. The parties of the left are anchored in this middle class, which also tends to include the workers in the modern key industries, as far as their attitudes are concerned. Almost two-thirds of the population are subjected to various degrees of marginalisation, to all kinds of exploitation, deprivation and humiliation.

The policy of the more far-sighted section of the oligarchy will be to maintain a vegetative existence for these people, with a view to securing their power that much longer. The country can be compared not only with Italy, but also with Iran, and then the horizon looks far more threatening. The marginalised masses around Teheran have decisively supported the Islamic turn against the *whole* model of Western bourgeois civilisation, against everything that is sacred to the good quarters of the cities of the Third World, these bridgeheads of the capitalist industrial system.

It is precisely in its capacity as a class living chiefly from rent that the oligarchy should naturally seek the opportunity for pacification, and use the state to administer a systematically differentiated corruption. True, those at the bottom will always receive too little to live on, and just too much not to die, yet in between there will be graduated rations. The question for us is whether our pressure will be merely sufficient to press them into this reformist orientation, or whether it will take the solution of the problems out of their hands, i.e. either driving their leaders politically offside in their own country, or chasing them off to Florida and the Rockies, where they've already taken the precaution of buying property for themselves.

If our political and ideological struggle has its centre of gravity in that third of society which has already arrived, we can only function in a reformist way. Sociological membership of the middle class, indirect dependence on rent and a state based on rent cannot offer a road to freedom. In that case, even our relationship to the working class will be primarily in the aspect in which it belongs to the privileged section of society, at least in certain branches. The corporatism of the trade unions is simply the expression of this. In the countries of dependent capitalism, and in view of the crisis of the world system as an *industrial* system, the alternative cannot be primarily based on the particular interests of the second industrial class.

Arnold Toynbee coined what I see as a very useful concept of the 'external proletariat', as distinct from the internal metropolitan proletariat. We can use this concept if we stress that the so-called elites in the peripheries in no way belong to it, but are rather for the most part a protusion and agency of the capitalist centre, while the external proletariat has a different structure from the internal one. In this case, without excluding the interests of the industrial workers, the centre of gravity will lie with those who, in terms of Marxist economic theory, are not yet 'really subsumed', i.e. the majority of the population who are marginalised to varying degrees and in varying ways.

As we were previously accustomed to burden the (metropolitan) proletariat with the interest of humanity, the world-historic mission, we are now perhaps inclined to completely abandon ascriptions of this kind. Yet it may well be worthwhile to investigate the connection between the immediate interests of the marginalised sections (and these are growing now also in the metropolises, if on a different scale) and the general interest of a humanity which has reached the earth's limits with its industrial capitalist expansion. Perhaps, to strike a variant on Marx, it is today *this* 'virgin soil of the people' which 'the lightning of thought'[32] must strike, and which must therefore be cultivated politically and ideologically.

There is no solution unless the people of the *ranchos* surrounding the cities and the people of the villages are organised to act for themselves. And if this is done, the alternative placed on the agenda will not be simply one *within* 'development', but an alternative *to* 'development', i.e. to industrialisation. One thing seems clear to me; after the experience of Soviet socialism, which in fact has not produced any socialism at all, anyone who seeks to copy in a dependent country entangled and underdeveloped by capitalism the same industrialisation that took place in the metropolises, favours the Soviet model whether intentionally or not (. . .)

If, as seems still the case with the strategy of historic compromise in Italy, the subjective ascent of the masses is ultimately subordinated to successful industrialisation, the fitness of national productive forces on the world market, this can only lead to statist bureaucracy. All that is then at issue is simply the greater or lesser efficiency of modernisation and the compensatory satisfaction of the masses for their perpetuated subalternity. Little is actually gained if a new team takes over responsibility for the export of oil, steel and aluminium, and for the big power stations. This is not dependent on the goodwill of a vanguard, but rather on the character of domination inherent to large-scale technology as such, not to speak of the constraints of the world market that pervade this.

We must learn that socialism cannot be the continuation of *this* industrial system, it must involve a break with it. *This* industrial system does not create the basic conditions for socialism, but leads us ever further away from its possibility. It will destroy 99 per cent of the country in which we live, and leave the majority of the population in slums on the last per cent. If the hope for the rise of the 'internal' European proletariat of the 19th century has been partially realised *as a result* of colonialism, this prospect is closed for the 'external' proletariat of the Third World, since there is no one else at whose expense this could be achieved. Even in the so-called threshold countries it is doubtful whether internal polarisation can be eliminated, precisely because the imported modern technologies marginalise more people than they employ.

On a world scale industrialisation *cannot* be achieved any longer, for the earth will not yield the material consumption of the North American middle class for the 10 or 15 billion people of the next century. And at the national level industrialisation can no longer solve any problems of *general* interest. As has been shown in the last decade — the so-called decade of development — industrialisation will only increase the sum of absolute impoverishment. The conclusion is to disengage, not for a better industrialisation but for a different type of civilisation, not for a later return to the world market but as an option for self-reliance, given that the world market must itself be forced into an involution.

The real alternative is not whether there is to be industry or not, but rather *what* means of production are suited to human beings. Science and technique can certainly be applied in a different direction, if there is a different society which shapes technology by its own standard, by the standard of the human beings who constitute it. This different society must first come into being before a different apparatus of production, productive in a different way, can be created out of the *elements* of science and technique, according to what serves the optimal development of the social individual. Efficiency and output per unit of time is *not* the criterion here.

What form could be a national solution take for those who are really the wretched of the earth? What should they therefore direct themselves towards? Shouldn't the inhabitants of the *ranchos* organise for something very similar to the Old Testament exodus from Egypt: an outbreak back to the countryside? What do we think for example of the forecast that Caracas in 20 years time will have 7 million inhabitants? Wouldn't it be better if people could learn to produce their means of subsistence cooperatively, independent of the blessings of agribusiness? They would build sound houses which people can live in with dignity. Schools and medical facilities would be organised communally. Simple reproduction would again be withdrawn as far as possible from the market. The extension of infrastructure (electricity, water supply, drainage and sanitation, means of communication and transport) would also have to be related to the needs of these communities instead of those of export industry. This naturally assumes that the land and natural resources are not just nationalised and made over to the state, but are socialised, i.e. returned to the disposal of those who use them communally. Ideas of this kind are often dismissed in our movement as romantic. Today, given that industrial progress is unsustainable on the old lines, different arguments must be found to reject them.

I would again like to stress that it is far less a question of a 'new socialism' than of new conditions of its realisation. The increasing readiness in our ranks to re-examine earlier goals has arisen from the experience that many things have happened in the world differently from how Marx, Lenin, etc. thought they would. Marx himself wrote in the *German Ideology* that communism is 'not a *state of affairs* which is to be established, an *ideal* to which reality [will] have to adjust itself', but rather 'the *real* movement which abolishes the present state of things'.[33]

For the decisive point I have to refer once again to the experience of 'actually existing socialism' that I already mentioned: the encroachment of the capitalist environment, the limited scope of the breakthrough against this which was originally aimed at. I recently discovered in Mexico how the reproach of Eurocentrism is easily incurred when you speak about the situation in the metropolises and assume this has something to do with conditions in the Third World. In my case, this would in fact be an 'East-Eurocentrism'. But we should distinguish between a Eurocentric fashion of discussion, which it is possible to slip into, and the actual situation in the metropolitan complex, the actual fact of its influence.

It is *not* because I now live in Western Europe, and am naturally as concerned for the possibilities of intervention there as I was previously in Eastern Europe, that I believe that nowhere in the world have we yet escaped the effects of the capitalist driving mechanism, which continues to have its motor and its most important fly-wheel in the metropolises. It is certainly no accident that precisely those economists who until a few years ago focussed their analyses particularly on the Third World have since turned their attention more sharply again to the centre. To put it more exactly, nowhere has escaped the *interaction* between metropolis and periphery within the one and only world economic context, which lies in the so far unstoppable process of capitalist accumulation.

We have precisely learned that the Russian revolution did not manage to break with the capitalist horizon of *development of the productive forces*. We have seen how right round the globe it is one and the same technology that has triumphed. Even the powerful voluntaristic effort that Mao Zedong undertook in order to preserve China from what in this sense is the 'capitalist road' proved unsuccessful. For what is the position with the 'four modernisations' that China is now striving to realise, if rather more slowly than a few years ago? The metropolitan model seems inescapable. Even those regions that once broke away from it tend to be re-integrated once again into the capitalist world market.

We used to be told that there were three allied forces attacking the capitalist system. First, the world socialist system; second, the working class, especially in the capitalist metropolises; and third, the national liberation movements. I don't intend to elaborate here how far wrong this was, simply to establish that it describes the situation in a totally false way. Is the popular movement in Poland the truth of the world socialist system? Are the social movements at the centre — the ecology movement against nuclear power stations, the women's movement against patriarchy, the movement of people seeking an alternative culture, a new spirituality, etc. — are these all movements of the revolutionary working class in disguise? Was the urban poverty that resulted from the destruction of the pre-capitalist economy and from capitalist marginalisation, and gave the Iranian revolution its decisive anti-American and anti-industrial impulse, what we had in mind when we spoke of national liberation movements?

The strategic meaning of this doctrine of three forces was for certain countries to break out of the world capitalist system and then oppose the entire periphery to it as an external power, through revolutions of liberation against the colonial system. The metropolitan proletariat was to collaborate as a third force from within, so as to bring capitalism/imperialism to its doom. All that is left of this is the sterile and highly dangerous confrontation of two blocs, the military pacts grouped around the two superpowers, which is tending to spread right across the globe and is waged on the backs of the poor nations. Today the question is again raised whether and how it is possible to overcome the system from within, since in the final analysis it doesn't have any 'outside'.

What seems clear enough is that the system can eventually be transformed only by the combined — and in a historic sense synchronised — action of the opposing forces in the entire First, Second and Third Worlds, and we must look to see whether there is not an objective convergence in the various lines of action, and if so, what this is, so that a mobilising hope can be placed on it and it can be consciously turned to use. But it is obviously no longer a question of metropolitan proletariat against metropolitan bourgeoisie, but rather — and here we are stuck in the face of the complexity of the social forces facing one another, a complexity which is not forseen in Marx's *Capital* and cannot simply be reduced to a two-front model. There evidently are other opposing forces than those we learnt about, at least forces that have to be defined differently, and vulgar sociology fails us if we want to understand them. One thing, however, they have in common: i.e. their struggle for self-determination against the material compulsions of the logic of accumulation, against what is ultimately the one and only world system of oppression, exploitation and alienation with its consequences through to physical annihilation.

Even if we leave aside the countries that call themselves socialist, and realistically consider the division between First and Third Worlds as a division *internal* to the capitalist world system, we can in no way make any theoretical progress if we try and mechanistically translate the old metropolitan class contradiction into an international one: world proletariat versus world bourgeoisie.

It is embarrassing to have to repeat something so self-evident. But where is the theory, where the proposal that could successfully replace this obsolete schema? If I see things correctly, we have on the one hand those global economic analyses that use a large-scale map of the world climate of capital accumulation to diagnose areas of depression and frontal system. Prediction in this case is always based on the paradigm of the distribution struggle. Where and in what branches will capital be invested in order to escape the fall in the rate of profit? Where will property be in danger? Where will impoverishment be exported to? If you remain at the level of economic analysis, this proves automatically to be economistic. For the call to struggle, if this can be heard at all, always has one and the same fatal flaw: it counsels acceptance of the capitalist rules of the game. Capital works according to the principle of quantity. As an echo of this, wage-labour — in its capacity as a component of capital — demands: 'We want more, more, more!' And this not only where the subsistence minimum has to be secured in this way, i.e. where exploited humanity is most severely impotent and suffering. The different life that people have to demand, the different civilisation, no longer comes into the picture. The unstoppable character of capital accumulation is internalised by theory.

On the other hand, we have detailed analyses of the social structure, its economic causes, the conditions of political struggle in particular countries. Here the dominant foreign influences always appear without their global context. There is something lacking in the mediation. It seems to me that this mediation, while it must also be established in the field of economic theory, should ultimately be sought in other dimensions of the social process. It is possible and necessary to investigate further the various forms in which capital subsumes labour-power. But the decisive provocation to revolt will come not from its curtailment of people's rights as labour-power, but rather from its curtailment of human rights and human dignity as such. It is not as wage-slaves but as human beings that people will rise up against the capitalist system.

We must refrain from directing our struggle chiefly for those graduated satisfactions that capital allows us according to its own logic, thus dividing our forces. For the wage-workers in Europe, at any rate, the question now is that they have to *emerge* out of their role *as* wage-labourers, as character-masks of the factor '*v*' for variable capital, as representatives of demands that are tied to this. This is the only way it is possible to combat the capitalist system as such and as a whole. Anyone who does not do this remains hopelessly bound to the vicious circle of rationalisation, export efficiency, competition between the monopolies, forced consumption and standardised life. Even a *political* struggle in the factories ultimately only drives the system in *its* direction.

Together with the exploited and oppressed of the Third World, we should struggle for the space in which they can refuse to conceive the good life after the style of Washington, London and Paris. This is a fata morgana, unreal and unattainable for everyone. Instead, we need a realistic plan for the construction of alternative contexts of work and living; this is far more crucial in the Third World than in the metropolises, yet even here more and more people are dropping out in this direction, without this being the result of any serious material pressures. If the radicalisation of the exploited and marginalised that is likely could be translated at first into practical attempts at a different way of life and the formation of autonomous communities, this might exert an attraction on others. And if at the same time pressure on the oligarchy, on the state, could extract a constructive response, a subsidising of socio-economic reconstruction. At the military and police centre which is unseizable the political process might then fluctuate between a reformist form and a revolutionary content. For the left this would mean familiarising itself with the idea of dropping out of bourgeois culture, in which they are themselves largely entangled, and moving on from reflection and de facto reformism to cultural-revolutionary practice. Cultural revolution is not less but more than political or social revolution; it embraces the other two, but right from the start proceeds differently and above all in a more deep-going way, in terms of a learning process by the masses themselves and in terms of their process of life. What I have in mind first of all is the ideological preparation for this turn.

This leads to one more point I would like to go into by way of conclusion. In its work for and with the marginalised sectors, the Marxist left will meet up with the best representatives of Christianity. These are the people who take seriously the idea of following Jesus, and it is possible to work together with them so as to overcome the paternalism unavoidable even in the liberators.

I have already spoken of an exodus from the *ranchos*. In 1790 Friedrich

Schiller wrote an essay titled 'The Mission of Moses', having in mind the problem of educating the German nation. In order to explain the problem the prophet faced, he described the state of the Hebrews in Egypt in the following words: 'the coarsest, most ill-natured, most rejected people on earth, made savage by three hundred years of neglect, rendered desperate and embittered by this long pressure of slavery, even in their own eyes humiliated, unnerved and crippled by a hereditary infamy' (leprosy) . . . Schiller was interested in how 'such an ignorant and crude bunch of herdsmen managed to achieve superiority over their refined oppressors'.[34]

The solution was to give this people identity and self-consciousness by an intense faith. This was only possible because Moses preached to them a true God — the conceptualised and idealised essence of the people, as Marx translated it — and preached this God by way of fable: i.e. adapted to the ill-developed powers of comprehension of the Hebrew tribes. I read with admiration how in the cautious and firm hand of Ernesto Cardenal the original text of the Gospel functioned for the peasants of Solentiname as a medium of revolutionary popular education, and as intensely as it did not despite but because of the spiritual message that illuminates it at every point. As far as I am aware, in the Catholic countries the Bible is little known. Perhaps we should help to spread the Gospel, the stories of the life of Jesus and Luke's history of the apostles. This is another *Communist Manifesto,* and between its lines, in its exegesis, there is space for everything that people need to know about capitalism.

In order to unite people thrown into slums, a programme is needed that points beyond the differences in their state of distress. This cannot be an abstract analysis, but only an appeal to their human claims, to their substance. And the equality of all human beings before God that Christ maintained in a world of slavery originally meant precisely this, not a consolation but a call to action. The struggle against discouragement, against degradation, against the destruction of human potential is the key to any socialist perspective. The rebellion in the shanty-towns can find its best form only in a movement of social-revolutionary awakening. This doesn't interest us Marxists, for we have a blind spot here in our tradition, inherited from the bourgeois Enlightenment. But we must help to organise it and give it political shape.

Our prejudices against Christianity, because we dislike the *Church,* we can set aside if we understand sufficiently well the situation of and within *parties* in power that we counted as belonging to our own movement, sometimes even parties which seem far away from power. The theology of liberation is proof that the original idea is breaking the ice of dead traditions, something that in our own case we unfortunately still hope for rather than actually experience. I am convinced that the two strands of emancipatory thought and faith, which historically are in any case aspects of a single process, are destined for reunification, and that we should do all that we can to accelerate this. The most important thing about the Italian strategy of historic compromise was that the Italian Communist Party sought to tackle the problem of the Catholic masses.

This problem, however, cannot be genuinely resolved at the level of mere considerations of alliance, which exclude the core of the ideological dimension. We should not be so indifferent towards faith as the Christian-Democrats of all countries, who handle the political business of the rich. In the social struggle, those who have a genuine, solidaristic faith generally find themselves fighting on the Christian side. So this must be a good cause. Almost every verse in the Gospel is a blow in the hypocritical face of the oligarchy, in the faces of all money-changers and high priests, pharisees and scribes of today, both within and outside of the Church. I see the amalgamation of socialists and Christians in practice *and* in ideas, the fusion of their emancipatory perspectives, as the key to the revolution in Latin America, and as an indispensable political element everywhere that religion takes a Christian form.

It seems to be also a lesson of the Iranian revolution that connections must be established *in advance,* projects integrated in advance, as far as this is possible. Iran is suffering today from the fact that the left there did not recognise the visage of the revolution in time, being still oriented to Western modernisation. At any rate, the reawakened Christianity of today bears far less of a threat in the form of the fanaticism and unhistoric regression accompanying the Islamic renaissance. The 'return of Christ' at the end of his second millenium could succeed at the level of the epoch. And we must try to take advantage of it if we are seeking — despite everything — to find the exit from capitalism.

In formative periods — and this is true not just for archaic times, but also for new cultural movements in the modern age — deeper strata of the social mind are mobilised than just economic and political interests in the narrower sense. At these levels, people's actions are generally still determined from outside by the prevailing system, even in their alternatives. If the point is not only to rise within given models of culture or civilisation, but to transform these very models — and this is the outstanding contemporary need, including a real change in needs themselves — then more non-determined individual energies must be released on a massive scale and brought together outside of all the existing institutions. These are energies which live in greater proximity to the core of the individual and exist in the tension between the ego — confined, yet conscious of its confinement — and the infinite claim that arises from the originally universal disposition of human nature. This was what Beethoven referred to in calling us: 'We finite creatures with the infinite spirit'.[35] This profound realm of our energy economy is the mental reality on which all religion has been based. If we understand this, it doesn't matter what name we give it. But this is where the impulse comes from for any collective cultural-revolutionary revolt as well as for any *conversion* in the practice of individual life. Our indispensable economic analyses and political programmes live and die according to whether they are able to mobilise these energies or not.

In terms of the Marxist tradition, the central question is the forces with which we seek to gain command of the Megamachine made up of objectified dead labour of all kinds, this being the overall product of capital accumulation and at the same time its crushing existence. Viewed anthropologically, dead labour is essentially dead spirit, 'objectified knowledge-power' as Marx himself called it. And the greatest part even of our living spirit and consciousness is only the reflection, determined from outside, of what we call the 'objective requirements' of the Great Machine. We cannot take a stand against it from these occupied regions of our consciousness. Marx's demand to overcome alienation, to establish the rule of living labour over dead, means that we should get into the stream of mental energy where this is still unoccupied, still without an alien burden, without dykes and defences. The association of these forces of living consciousness is the most general and fundamental condition for liberation.

Expanded version of a talk given in Caracas, May 1981

Reply to Three Questions from the West German Radio

What is Peace?

Peace is the ideal condition in which human beings do not use violence against one another — not even concealed and indirect violence — so that each person can develop according to the average potential of the time. So it also includes freedom and justice, and equality between human beings.

At first glance this looks too broad. Won't we be happy just to be spared being killed by atom bombs, not to mention 'conventional' shells? Or if we can end the situation in which every year more children die of hunger in the Southern half of the earth (14 million in 1980) than died each year of the Second World War? Or if our oxygen supply is not rapidly exhausted?

But shall we escape all these things if we simply continue in the old way? We have shown the whole world what and how much one needs to have. How can things improve if more and more people on our finite earth each consume, destroy and poison more and more, after our own model? In this way we shall inevitably come into conflict both with one another and with nature.

We don't like hearing people repeat that 'there have always been wars . . . ' But this is all too true. If the Third World War is not to break out, if half of humanity is not to die of hunger, if the final collapse of the environment is to be avoided — then we must raise ourselves above the laws of human history as these have been known up till now.

The first thing to learn, and not just in military affairs, is that security and peace are not the same thing. If you seek security, you practise distrust and take precautions which in turn feed the mistrust of the other side. It is quite clearly a policy of *security* that has led to the situation where we are now sitting on a nuclear powder-keg. The other side is supposed to be deterred by threat. Its own missiles are accordingly deployed just as carefully with the same aim in mind. A policy of *peace* would remove or at least reduce the threat, confident that this would also remove or at least reduce the threat to ourselves. Anyone who claims to pursue peace and security together is deceiving their listeners. What has up to now been called security really means suicide.

Yet it is not enough to prevent the latest missiles, even to abolish the whole arsenal so that it doesn't abolish us. If the goal is only this and no more, it will not be achieved. You can't defeat a hydra by chopping off one or two of its heads, if its internal juices are still producing new ones. If we want to cut open the monster's belly so that it really does perish, we must first of all know its name.

The monster is our industrial system, our industrial way of life itself. It is no accident that we have come to the present pass. It is simply our skill in changing nature that is now showing its cloven hoof. At one time we had great success in producing our basic means of subsistence. Since then we have been repeating ourselves on an ever greater scale, after the Olympic motto: 'Higher, further, faster, better!' — above all: *Always* more.'

It was here in Europe that we found the *non plus ultra*, the economic system with the strongest impulse and most frightful efficiency, which we are so proud of. In 1860 the English trade-unionist Thomas Joseph Dunning wrote:[36]

Capital is said . . . to fly turbulence and strife, and to be timid, which is very true; but this is very incompletely stating the question. Capital eschews no profit, or very small profit, just as Nature was formerly said to abhor a vacuum. With adequate profit, capital is very bold. A certain 10 per cent will ensure its employment anywhere; 20 per cent certain will produce eagerness; 50 per cent positive audacity; 100 per cent will make it ready to trample on all human laws; 300 per cent, and there is not a crime at which it will scruple, nor a risk it will not run, even to the chance of its owner being hanged.

This is clear from all the curves of economic growth, which from 1750 no longer rise imperceptibly, as before, but suddenly start to point vertically upwards, so that it is unnecessary to attribute the production of weapons to a special profit interest. There is this, of course, but more is involved. In the past, those who hoped to solve all problems by expropriation had no intention of stopping the Great Machine. The capital-relation is not the ultimate cause of expansion, but only its most recent means. It is simply the highest branch on the tree of human modes of production, and it will prove quite impossible to saw it off and leave all else untouched.

Peace requires that we make a new start with the whole of civilisation, at least partly blocking the sources of competition for scarce material goods by reducing all material consumption and all material production to the minimum necessary for an approximately equal satisfaction of basic natural needs. Goethe had his Faust say: [37]

> Full well I know the earthly round of men,
> And what's beyond is barred from human ken;
> Fool, fool is he who blinks at clouds on high...
> This world will not be mute to him of worth.

As his last effort Faust therefore drains a marshland so that 'millions may possess this space'. What now, when this work is accomplished?

It seems the only prospect open is 'beyond', 'upwards', 'within' and of course towards other people. And the reason we must focus our energies in *this* direction is that it is dangerous to life to go on changing nature so much, piling up knowledge for this end and storing up treasure in the process. Halt! No further! Every new investment is diabolic and deadly, not only investment in missiles. Peace begins with abandoning the greater part of the work most of us do every day. Naturally, demolition and reconstruction will take some time. But though the pyramids remain, no one is living there any more.

What Can You Do Personally For Peace?

It is worth mentioning here that I don't have a car, for example; I have moved into an apartment which is the smallest possible for my work; I eat only a little meat, as every portion contains enough grain to fill five or more people. Unfortunately, all this is initially more of symbolic than of practical significance. What seems to me more important: I am prepared to live without any kind of 'protection' through weapons. I find this easier in so far as the strategists have convinced me that their only defence would kill me in the process.

When it comes to political battles, I try to argue patiently and fairly. For example, I wrote to Franz-Josef Strauss asking if he would be prepared to hold a public debate with me in one of the smaller Bavarian cities on the theme of 'Europe Without Nuclear Weapons — Could We Be Blackmailed?' Passau would do, as I've already come across Strauss there.

In the last instance our power to convince other people depends on a way of acting that shows readiness for peace, but this is not easy to practise. I have found that I can myself be sharp and intolerant particularly within the left, when I hear outmoded recipes put forward which I am sure are wrong and lead nowhere, or when resistance after the fashion of the Red Army Fraction is recommended.

As someone who knows the dogmas of the left inside out, I was seldom so touched as on the day when I heard the news, in East Germany, that foi me meant: They have killed Ulrike Meinhof. Now I would like to say to those who find themselves in Ulrike's last footsteps, or are toying with such ideas: You are ultimately helping those who killed her. But if I put it so bluntly, and am angry into the bargain, then of course I can't get through to them. And who is to bring them back, if not those in the peace movement who have decided on non-violence, rationally and on the basis of their particular mental constitution?

Given that I wrote my book *The Alternative* in the GDR while continuing my professional work, it is easy for me to spend the whole day here reading, thinking, writing and speaking in pursuit of the goals of the ecology and peace movement. I feel responsible for making the best use possible of these favourable conditions.

I am at present working on a book together with Michaela von Freyhold, a colleague at Bremen University, which I am also attached to. We are putting forward proposals for the policy of the peace movement. Michaela lived and worked for almost ten years in Africa, and I was 30 years in the GDR. So we are bringing together our experiences of the three worlds in order to see how Europe — West *and* East — could become nuclear-free and bloc-free, not least of course Germany.

Peace Today? Don't You Have a Feeling of Impotence and Resignation?

Impotence is less dependent on the magnitude of the danger than on the experience of being able to do nothing against it. Don't most people succumb to resignation because they are afraid to put up what resistance is possible? They fear the immediate risk more than the eventual one? Just recall the time of resistance to Hitler. How little the citizens of this country would need to risk today in order to bring about very fundamental changes! They needn't all practise civil disobedience. If instead of a single demonstration in Bonn we had mass demonstrations by the citizens of every town, we would soon manage to dispense with nuclear weapons and NATO.

Those who dare not take any risk fail to realise, perhaps deliberately, that the apocalypse is highly probable unless we reckon with it in all seriousness and act accordingly. Essentially the apocalyptic situation gives me courage, as it obviously does a large section of young people. Why else do the young people who feel they have no future demonstrate and protest so resolutely? We *have* to find a way out, and we must therefore try unconditionally, so that in the worst case it will not be our responsibility. In Germany this is *the* moral lesson from the Hitler time. I have recently heard similar things from the older generation.

We don't imagine it will be easy to catch two birds in the bush. We only know that the one we have in the hand is absolutely no use to us this time. The goal we have to achieve is like seeking to bring an avalanche to a halt from within. If someone could see it from outside, it would look as if this avalanche was braked and halted shortly before impact by a spiritual hand. This is against the law of the inert mass of concrete and steel that encases us. So it has to be an effort that comes from consciousness, from the soul, so concentrated and by so many people that there has been no historical parallel.

We must see ourselves somewhat after the fashion of the exodus from Egypt inspired by Moses, or the first Pentecost after Christ's ascension — combined into one, and on a scale embracing the whole of humanity, though starting in the rich countries and particularly in Europe. For we were the sorcerer's apprentice who first called the broom to life; it is we whom everyone else copies; the vicious circle has its centre here and it is our continent that is the most vulnerable.

I believe this *conversion* is possible, because now humanity feels threatened in its drive for self-preservation. The tendency is growing, and it is a tendency inherent in every human being, to entrust ourselves to an extreme alternative, however uncertain — because there is nothing else left to do. This decision can suddenly take hold of millions — tomorrow or the day after — and expand the horizon of political possibility overnight. Relatively small or medium catastrophes will not fail to remind us how near the hour is.

I propose that in expectation of this moment each of us should encourage disquiet and the readiness for a general change of heart, both in ourselves and in our own milieu. Let us withdraw more than just our vote from the Great Machine and its servants. We must completely cease playing along with it wherever this is possible. We must gradually paralyse everything that goes in the old direction: military installations and motorways, nuclear power stations and airports, chemical factories and big hospitals, supermarkets and education works.

Let us consider how we can feed ourselves, keep warm, clothe ourselves, educate ourselves and keep ourselves healthy independent of the Great Machine. Let us begin to work at this before the Great Machine has completely regulated us, concreted us over, poisoned us, asphyxiated us and sooner or later subjected us to total nuclear annihilation.

We must live differently in order to survive! Then we can perhaps still arrive where we have always wanted to, if only with one string of our heart: at a peace that is something higher than all the reason contained in our previous history.

1981

Who Can Stop the Apocalypse? Or the Task, Substance and Strategy of the Social Movements

So as not to cause any misunderstanding, I must confess right away that this cannot be, and is not supposed to be, a talk by an objective observer. It is more of an appeal than an analysis, and in its form it is more of an outline sketch than a scientific lecture. The first reason for this is a practical one — both trivial and welcome. In the last two years I have not been able to undertake scientific work in the strict sense, as too much has been going on outside the libraries. This already bears on the subject of my talk. A movement is under way in various countries of Protestant central and northern Europe, a movement which I like to call the ecology *and* peace movement, but which by virtue of its inherent dynamic is a movement for conversion in the metropolises, for a transformation that goes right through to the material and mental foundations of our culture. This movement is at a formative stage, and naturally corresponds with similar tendencies in all other parts of the world. My interest in this subject is not academic, but existential, so I shall deal with it in a quite one-sided and absolutist manner. In this case, too, the universities are not the major source from which the movement proceeds. The present time is one of applied theory, or to be more accurate, applied ideology.

Basically, the question at issue is still more elementary. For many people, the exterminist and self-destructive tendency that seems to have taken hold of our social body presents itself in so fundamental and necessary a way that the evidence for it is as great as was the evidence for the compelling myths of archaic times. Even though the outlines of the goal are quite unclear, nothing needs to be demonstrated or proved.For the plagues of ancient Egypt are upon us, the horsemen of the apocalypse can be heard, the seven deadly sins are visible all around us in the cities of today, where Babel is multiplied a thousandfold. In 1968 the promised

Canaan of general emancipation appeared on the horizon, and this time at last for women as well. But almost all of those who believe in this have tacitly come to realise that first of all will come the years in the wilderness. All that is lacking now is the pillar of fire to show us the route of our exodus.

This is all to say that a mood is spreading which is more to be grasped in the language of these old parables than by scientific analysis of behaviour, and which is gradually making its way across all the differentiations that political economy, sociology, political science and social psychology like to maintain. And this mood has more reason than ever before to be apocalyptic, this time not just for one particular tribe, one or other particular state or even one particular civilisation, but rather for the one civilisation that is finally decisive. This I assume is self-evident. I don't intend to prove anything, to present the evidence for those who don't want to read the writing on the wall, as I believe that facts and arguments are not what such people lack.

This will make clear my basic attitude towards the subject of this congress, and the counterposing of 'governments' and 'movements' — something that I find very appropriate, as by this complementarity both concepts attain a very global and comprehensive character. So that it is experience rather than logically presented arguments that lead me to ask what is meant by the 'future of politics'. Shouldn't futurologists assume that politics has to be put in cold storage? You can of course say that movements are also political. What I want to stress though is that *professional* politics is not going to save anything, but can only make everything worse. Hopeful initiatives cannot come from this direction, unless they are spurious. It wasn't really the German chancellor who brought the USA and the Soviet Union to the conference table in Geneva. And besides, what are we to expect of this? On any question of survival, it always comes down to forcing the politicians to react by irresistible pressure. Thus everything depends on convoking 'non-political' or 'extra-political' forces, precisely on an overwhelming movement of conversion, which disrupts the normal activity of the official institutions, for example the activity of the defence ministries in 'securing peace'.

Let us assume that a peace research team was to observe the present scene in Western Europe, Japan and the USA in order to make a prognosis. They would naturally recognise a dialectic, an interaction, between the grass-roots movements and the forces that speak for these in the institutions. And if they were optimistic, they would conclude that what ultimately matters is that parliaments and governments should make new decisions, given that a new security policy is a matter for the state, it has the state as its subject. I would not challenge any of this. This is at least one aspect of the process. It is clear theoretically that movements and institutions do somehow or other interact, that if a movement is successful it will transform the institutions, and in some way or other will be itself institutionalised, etc. This is just common sense.

Yet for reasons that have nothing to do with any general theory, as is sometimes put forward to relate movements and institutions, I would say that only the peace movement can save our civilisation. And by the peace movement here I am putting the part for the whole. Given this very particular extreme situation in which we find ourselves, I mean that against all the institutions that have been programmed for whole epochs to pursue everything in the accustomed direction, or at least to maintain everything as it is, only the most basic social movements can bring about that break in cultural continuity without which we shall be unable to save our very existence. The more this movement proceeds from the grass roots, the more decisively it raises the question of power. Not in the sense of preparing to storm the Winter Palace. Its main subversive potential is that of destroying the traditional consensus that supports the state and constructing a new consensus, and in this connection the front line generally runs right through the individuals concerned. But as this movement criticises the old world order in its totality, it naturally negates for a start its whole institutional heaven. Here it polarises against all those instances that make up this old heaven, and thus also against the traditional opposition.

We already fall back into the system if we act as if politics could be challenged by politics (of the same type). What can we achieve by immersing ourselves in the study of how the dominant politics functions, even with a view to bringing about improvements? The time always comes when the thinkers of a new era refuse to get drawn into the distinctions of scholasticism. We still run the danger of getting absorbed by the 'compulsion of things' which is administered and reproduced on an expanded scale, just like a certain Green parliamentarian in the Federal Republic. This person used to radically oppose nuclear power stations. Then he got elected to the *Landtag*. He soon realised that a nuclear power station could be built even against his opposition. So he transformed himself into a realist and began discussing whether an underground power station — if such could be built! — wouldn't be better than an above-ground one. As if there weren't already enough reformists to take on that role. So the system easily gobbled him up.

This strikes me as an example of the problem of the relationship between science and the system on the one hand, science and the movement on the other. Should we not say goodbye to this contemplative analysis of the decisive objects? You can either be a servant and adviser of various governments and other system-maintaining institutions, or be militantly for the movement and in the movement. I am not advocating fanaticism, or even a break in communication. Yet debate will be more honest if it is conducted between intelligent people on either side, and not through so-called 'intermediaries' who express themselves in non-partisan translation. The point is to see the praxis that alone can save us as running completely across the traditional business of politics and science, also across the political advisers of the left, who generally produce only few initiatives that do not contribute to the prolonging of existing conditions.

We cannot expect any escape from the vicious circle in which our civilisation is terminally trapped from the kind of science, aiming to master its object, that we have had since Euclid, Socrates, Aristotle and Archimedes, simply because this is fundamentally bound up with this civilisation's motive forces. As far as the social process is concerned, its objectivity stands for the subjugation to laws which can only wreck our evolution if we do not manage to overcome them.

Let us assume we were living at the time when one of the many Central American civilisations that produced steadily growing pyramids was in its death-throes. Would it be sensible to expect help from those very priests who represented the law by which that culture was born and grew up, then blossommed, declined and died? The science business is largely the priestly corporation of our present civilisation. Most likely, every means it hits upon, every advice it gives, will only mean adding a further stone to our tower of Babel, for example in the shape of a new industry for environmental protection. Of course I am speaking of those scientists who play their role and uphold the rules that have to be overthrown if anything is to be left of our civilisation except — in the best of cases — pyramids of reinforced concrete, which don't even keep their shape as long as stone ones do.

Even that supposedly progressive economic analysis which uses Marxist categories functions today in conformity with the system. It goes on feeling the pulse of a still continuing accumulation of capital, calculates profit rates and forecasts short-term — and recently also long-term — cyclical crises. But it has nothing more to say on the question of how this pulse is to be stopped, how the accumulation of capital can be not just measured but actually brought to an end. All that is left is the latest economistic reformism, which already assumes the next long wave, the breakthrough into eco- and bio-industries, total cable communication, etc. as an inadvertible given which we have to surrender and adapt ourselves to. They don't even ask whether there is a chance of halting accumulation in its present trough.

In practice as well as in theory, the old left forms part of the institutional order that has to be overcome, and for this reason the movement of conversion is also directed against *its* mental structure. Though Marxist theory did not originally raise the task of stopping accumulation, it suggests that capitalist accumulation will come to a halt for intrinsic reasons, as a consequence of the internal contradictions of the bourgeois mode of production, whereas it is becoming ever more probable that the avalanche of accumulation is catastrophically reaching external limits — and without encountering fundamental resistance from the specific interests of the subordinate classes. Quite the contrary. Yet for the traditional analysis the new social movements serve only as a preliminary substitute, behind whose action the real protagonists will again re-appear.

This is failing to see the wood for the trees. Today the provocation proceeds from the reproduction process as a whole, or rather from its ever less controllable dysfunctions. It is the all-pervasive *output*, harmful in the most varied ways, against which resistance is developing. The exterminist consequence that is inherent in the entire mode of production acts against human nature on the whole scale of values from the highest ideals of self-realisation down to mere self-preservation. It is not abstract causes, but concrete sufferings, that produce the counter-mobilisation. No matter which way the individual experiences this injury, the psyche reacts as a whole, and the movement provides a synthesis for the impression that no treatment for the symptom is any longer of use.

This leads to a new, or rather a very old, answer to the question of the mode of association. Should the opposition forces base their unity on a compromise between their differing social interests, or should they locate this unity above or below the level of differences of economic interest, i.e. at the level of fundamental and long-term interests? If we believe the latter, however, we depart from what in the traditional view is the most important thing: class interests in the stricter sense. We completely cease to consider the analysis of the social structure as the main key to a transforming practice. We give primary status to *other* differentiations (in particular social-psychological ones) within the social continuum of interests.

The distinction between fundamental and long-term interests on the one hand, and immediate and short-term interests on the other, becomes more important than the distinction of different class interests. Within the metropolitan countries, which have as a whole an exploiting position, the class contradiction has only a relative importance, and is always based on immediate and short-term interests; as a general rule it fuels the characteristic dynamic of material expansion. In the movement, on the other hand, those forces come together which want to abolish the overall system of regulation by which all phenomena of crisis are mediated. It goes without saying that we expect these forces to develop a plan that takes into account among other things the continuing class differentiation, and prevents redistribution against the interests of the wage-earners from raising still further the threshold for the leap into a different logic. It is simply a question here of a change in the key position given to the traditional social question.

This has all been preliminary — perhaps in too great detail — so as to make my premises clear. I admit that I am using an extremely global construction. I started — in the title — by speaking of a number of social movements (and I don't deny their plurality). Then I went on to speak of the ecology *and* peace movement as a single movement. And this phenomenon does exist, or is beginning to exist, in Holland and Germany for example (even a little in the GDR), with signs appearing also here in Scandinavia. In actual fact, however, even in these countries we find a diversity of movements, and the women's movement or the squatters' movement — just to take two examples — would in many cases politely decline inclusion in this general concept that exists in my head. Which is why I took refuge in a yet wider field, and spoke of a movement for conversion in the metropolises.

This naturally contains right away a whole number of implicit and venturesome assumptions. Let us take two of the metropolitan countries, France and Germany. It would be hard to find two European countries with more different political cultures. But I would maintain that in the German resistance to the nuclear power station at Whyl and the resistance in France to the new military training ground at Larzac, the two peoples are closer in spirit than in their political structures, as close in fact as the French jacquerie was to the German peasant war, even though the two were separated by 200 years. I believe there is a subterranean current at work here.

To give another example, why has this peace movement risen up within one year first in Europe, then in Japan, then in North America? And the uprising in Poland, which didn't talk especially about peace, but like every popular revolution dealt with *everything,* did even more than our West European demonstrations towards the cause of peace, by forcing one of the two military blocs into a political impasse. Real movements are converging in this way, even though their origin and their specific goals lie wide apart — so that in the final analysis it is perhaps not so arbitrary for me to consider them together.

As far as my construction goes, it is global not only in the figurative sense but also literally — just like the challenge. Conversion in the metropolises: where are these metropolises? Firstly, of course, the European countries, as well as those from North America to Australia where the Europeans wiped out the indigenous inhabitants. And then of course Japan, which was so strikingly well disposed to assimilate the aggressive spirit of European industrialism. But where in the Third World today are there not big cities that are bridgeheads of the capital accumulation that proceeds from the centre? Industrialisation in the East also obeys the same imperatives, not only since it's got in debt to finance capital. The global metropolis has no geographical limits, it is this so far unstoppable process of industrial expansion driven and guided by capital, which is driving us over the edge of the abyss at a hundred points simultaneously.

It is this challenge — Edward Thompson has termed it exterminism, referring initially to its military side, but this can easily be generalised — which gives the diversity of movements a tendency to unite in a single movement of conversion. In the final analysis — but I don't mean this in the abstract sense, it will show itself in practice! — the marginalised masses in the countries of the Third World who plug into the electric power supply without paying will prove to be convergent with the movement against nuclear power stations, even though in functional terms they seem totally in contradiction. The question is simply that the capitalist industrial system can only be driven back and destroyed by an ungraspable and manifold movement of humanity, without formal coordination, not by an industrial working class that is defined in purely economic terms and centrally organised.

As human beings we are all marginalised, it is just that many of us are not yet aware of it. Many people still say, in pacifying terms, that the Megamachine is ultimately made up of human beings. Sure! But here the reversal of the relation of master and slave has been achieved on the grandest scale. Does anyone still seriously imagine that the old actor Ronald Reagan is only the master of the Doomsday machine which he's been transported into? But the marginalised and excluded, those with their backs against the wall, now have an unbeatable ally in this very wall that they have their backs against. This wall is formed by the limits of the earth itself, against which we really shall be crushed to death if we do not manage to brake and bring to a halt the Great Machine that we have created before this finally bumps against it. Every action that somehow or other obstructs its progress forms part of the movement, a progress which is above all the progress of its investments and the acquisition of capital for these. In the rich countries in particular, we are all in the situation of the building worker who lives next to the planned new airport runway and is offered work on it. He has to make a new decision!

How can we bring to an end the industrial era, an era that cannot endure in the long run as it is consuming its own foundations, before such time as it dies from its own activity and takes us with it? This is the question that demands an answer. This answer must lie in concrete actions, not only political ones. Its tendency — at first a symbolic one — will be to tear down the tower of Babel before this collapses upon us. And the resolution for this must be defended against any demand to say first of all what better system we want to replace it with. At the time of the anti-fascist struggle, Bertold Brecht told 'The Buddha's Parable of the Burning House', which is very relevant here. When the roof was already burning, someone inside

> Asked me what it was like outside, whether it wasn't raining
> Whether the wind wasn't blowing perhaps, whether there was
> Another house for them, and more of this kind.

and the Buddha answered:

> ... Truly, friends
> Unless a man feels the ground so hot underfoot that he'd gladly
> Exchange it for any other, sooner than stay, to him
> I have nothing to say ...   [38]

We are not yet in a position to tear down the tower. Investments now in progress are not only reinforcing the floors already built, they are massively at work building the next storey. And our efforts to halt this growth are only fragmented: we demonstrate against a particular weapons system, we prevent a nuclear power station here, an airport runway there. In most cases we only delay things. We reduce the speed limit on the motorways a little. But we have to persist.

We need at least to consider a great moratorium, a kind of general strike against expansion, the blocking of everything embraced by the word 'development', a pull on the emergency brake. This is the task that the conversion movement has to fulfil above all else, in a whole variety of forms. It must actually achieve the stopping of investment that hostile propaganda already attributes to it, by directing itself even more against sales expectations than against the bulldozers and concrete mixers.

Liberation from deadly, injurious and superfluous labour is the other side of this anti-investment strategy. Even though emancipation is not the immediate slogan here, it is exactly at this point that the possible gain in freedom is to be found. The industrial system and its implications oppress freedom, and not only at the centre. Almost all peoples who have submitted themselves to a forced industrialisation in the hope of finding freedom at the end of the tunnel have remained stuck at its darkest point. Contrary to a once current idea, freedom is not obtainable through industrialisation, but in fact only through the rejection of industrialisation. It is pertinent here, of course, that there is in fact no other industrial system than the capitalist one, and that we certainly deceived ourselves in seeing the ultimate cause of its alienation in the capitalist *form* of industrial progress. Industrialisation has since already shown that it can no longer offer any perspective of emancipation simply because it is impossible for all peoples to achieve. And it has to be halted here in Europe above all, where the industrial system had its start, and where we are particularly susceptible, as also is Japan, to its unforeseen backlash. Unilateral industrial 'disarmament', or at least the transition to a quite different kind of equipment, is the motto here.

Now it is one thing to recognise something like this as a task, even to welcome it. But is it at all possible for human beings to halt a historical dynamic in which they are themselves so deeply enmeshed? Isn't a conversion movement of this kind simply a mere postulate, corresponding in reality to nothing more than an incommensurable sum of isolated fears and hopes? Won't we all continue to be hurled along on the roundabout? After all, I myself travelled here by plane.

In my view, the problem is more specific. For there have already been several movements of conversion in history, precisely in times of crisis which were not completely dissimilar to our own. These have always worked with free energies, i.e. energies not tied down in the given institutional context, and in this connection it is not just a matter of counting heads and working out from people's occupations where energies are free and where they are tied. Many people divide their forces. There really are such free energies; the substance is there. That 'one-dimensionality' which Marcuse warned against is even now incomplete. Alternative movements of this kind, for this is what they always were, have succeeded and failed in different ways and to different degrees, i.e. it is impossible to definitively conclude from studying them whether the present effort will be victorious or not. And yet previous crises were always local in character, and the concrete barriers that such movements sought to overcome were not of so absolute a kind as today. These movements didn't run up against factors that are bound up with the very existence of society.

Considered superficially, what is now rapidly crumbling in the Federal Republic is simply the post-War consensus. Generalising a bit beyond the edge of the national stage, it is the fourth Kondratiev wave that is particularly reaching its end in our part of the world, where the population enjoyed a rise in welfare as a substitute for their lost identity. But beneath this lies the end of the perspective of industrial progress in general; even if a new wave of industrialisation is possible, it no longer promises anything, but is simply more threatening (for example, it is even more essential to ban genetic technology than nuclear). The industrial revolution, however, presupposed the Renaissance, and the Renaissance even in name presupposed Graeco-Roman civilisation. The oldest stratum of civilisation involved in the present crisis is that of patriarchy, with ten millenia behind it.

The very complexity and relative indirectness of the answer already shows that all these superimposed formations are forms that overlay a relatively constant substance, the species-nature of the human being, which is not a product of history, but of natural history. Something that has gradually proceeded from this is now reacting upon it, striking through all the superimposed historical strata down to the original basis. All those human energies involved in the evolution of civilisation find themselves more or less implicated in the overall exterminist tendency.

Since this cannot be an accidental result, the correction must also get to the roots. The movement of conversion today must precisely bring about a mutation in the 'genotype' of society. The theologian Johann Baptist Metz called this an anthropological revolution. What does this relate to? European civilisation has certainly discovered the *non plus ultra* of efficiency (as its admirers call it) in expanded reproduction. But very probably this realises only in an excessive measure something that is present already in our species endowment.

Doesn't the whole progress that led into civilisation have above all the character of *material* expansion (more heads, more consumption per head)? Even in the earliest religions, aren't the intelligible, the mental forces ultimately deployed for the sake of mastering the *external* world? And isn't the centre of gravity of all human culture to be found in these 'exosomatic organs', from the stone flint to the computer? People nowadays speak of the 'exo-centredness' of human nature, quite analogously to the understanding that the ant has its essence not in itself, but in the ant colony as a whole. Whatever previous movements of conversion may have changed, they have not affected this basic text. The next prophet in line has had to begin again by preaching against the normal social life of his time.

In my opinion, we can make clear what the problem is by reference to the ants. If human nature was so involved with the social edifice right from the start as is the case with the ants, there would be no possibility of escape from the blind alley of evolution. As ants, we could not even raise the question of putting our cultural evolution into reverse or correcting it, after it had led us into the Babylonian captivity of our technostructure. As human beings, we are far too ready to agree that we are only ants and as little capable as other species of escaping from an evolutionary impasse, withdrawing from a specialisation that has prospects only in the short term.

Is this really impossible? With our genotype it should be possible. Our cultural specialisation is precisely not biologically inscribed. The ten thousand years of civilisation have not made us incapable, at least not yet, of living without our artificial environment. As opposed to the ant, human individuals are in a position, in certain circumstances which at times are present on a massive scale, of withdrawing the most significant portion of their natural powers from the social edifice and engaging them in new purposes. And there are historic examples for the reconstruction or demolition of enchaining structures, for their disintegration, even for an exodus from them.

If the exosomatic evolution is to be corrected, this is only conceivable with a force not yet disposed of, or at least not yet decisively disposed of, by the civilisation stamped by the last ten thousand years of history. Our genotype is such a force, and it does not doom us to carry round this technostructure like a tortoise its shell. This is a force, and the only force, that stands outside the given historical universe, and yet is a real social force that can be summoned up within society. Human beings are indeed already social beings when they enter into this history, which presents itself, or is recorded as, a history of class struggles. At this point in time they have all the essential capacities and desires that drive them through to today. And as it appears, they have since this point in time become alienated in many respects from their definition, by following the principle that in the Bible is referred to as Mammon.

Before going on, I want to mention one thing, though I only have an intimation here. As I see it, the genotype is that social power present in every human being which the old prophets always evoked under the name of God. God is the alter ego, the 'thou' of our genotype that is always aimed at. The place of God is where the developmental needs of our original nature converge, above all of course an inward place. This is why we can be called from and to this place.

I see in this completely this-sided and inner-worldly connection the reasons why the religious dimension is now making its return, and the fundamental role it has to play. What religions invariably and timelessly say about God and his/her 'actions' and 'attitudes', the way s/he 'proceeds', seems to me to be directly a pattern containing all those models by which the task, substance and strategy of the conversion movement can be described. Here there are readily translatable categories in order to grasp what I have in mind as the extra- or suprahistorical saving power, the substance which bears the concrete and then of course completely historical action.

The decisive thing will be the amount of energy that we bring together. This is on the one hand the problem of associating the unbound energies, their bundling together, for which the old political forms are inadequate. More precisely, the question is really that these energies should be at work on all sides, or decentrally, and in the same direction, so that the system they are confronting cannot deploy its forces now here, now there, but is simply overburdened. Coordination is above all else communication, knowledge of one another and also feeling the connecting stream. On the other hand, there is the problem of releasing as many as possible of those energies still tied into the system. The genotype is certainly there, but its best forces may be expropriated and alienated.

The energy it can supply in its own interest is quite other than constant. Here it is above all the association also experienced in actions, the social-psychological support, that gives endurance to the new distribution of mental resources.

As far as *strategy* goes, the strategy that will result from this in the historic context, I will confine myself here to the narrower field of the conversion movement in the metropolises, where the securing of human dignity generally doesn't begin with the struggle for a minimal existence. I am completely aware that we are working here in conditions of luxury, that a social network covers our uprising which would have difficulty in existing without colonialism. What I have to say is also much abbreviated and incomplete.

The basis, as already mentioned, is the progressive disintegration of the social body, as expressed in a decay of the system of values and thus of all institutional authorities. More and more people are either excluded, marginalised, dismissed, or directly motivated to drop out, with either all or part of their energies. This gives rise by necessity to a strategy (by which I don't mean anything like a secretly elaborated and planned plot) that combines two elements: a gradually spreading *refusal* and a deliberate *obstruction*. This is not meant as a kind of new discovery, I simply want to draw attention to what is necessary and deliberate in it.

Refusal, above all, means protecting one's own energies from being absorbed, and on top of this it means active withdrawal of energies from the ruling structures, very often backed by an accusation. Refusal of military service through to total non-cooperation is the most striking example of it. I believe that non-political withdrawal is only a temporary moment in this context. One may say that the productive apparatus itself rejects people's energies — unemployment — and that the hippies, alternative people, job-sharers, etc. only help to relieve its burden. But a far more comprehensive trend is involved, also with those who for the time being still remain 'inside'. It is already affecting work motivation as such.

At the political level refusal means the withdrawal of legitimation. The *Frankfurter Rundschau* of 12 May 1982 quoted a study according to which 66 per cent of young people in North-Rhine Westphalia, and 43 per cent of adults in the Federal Republic as a whole, denied that politicians took decisions in the interest of the people. Still more people are convinced that the big enterprises think only of their profits and not of the well-being of society. 74 per cent of young people in North-Rhine Westphalia and 46 per cent of adult citizens in the whole country recognise — naturally enough given their assessment of the causes — the increasing tendency to resolve conflicts by violence. This means that the system is already near to defeat ideologically.

The crisis of legitimation naturally finds expression also in elections, as the preferred ritual of legitimation. The counter-movement will either boycott elections and/or gain a political foothold in parliament that is conceived right from the start as being there simply to disrupt the normal execution of the 'compulsion of things', to tear away the curtain of justification and expand the space for extra-parliamentary forces to put pressure on the institutions.

Obstruction means restricting the operation of the system by active resistance, starting with the most dangerous of its normal directions of development. The motto for this is selective ungovernability. Specific measures such as the installation of new weapons systems, the construction of nuclear power stations, more and more airports, motorways, new industrial plant, etc. should be made impossible. Actions can stretch from blockades and demonstrations via refusal of taxes to legal obstructions, making each new investment a wearying obstacle course. The most important thing, however, is the relativising of the norms of an achievement society, the undermining of the consensus for expansion.

The administrators of the Great Machine and their advisers stress the fact that our super-complex society cannot tolerate the shock of disorganisation. Chaos and anarchy must be avoided. What purpose these slogans have, and how relative their truth-content is, has been shown by the political struggles in Poland. Those who demand that the movement should provide detailed recipes for reconstruction in advance can be answered with the words of Goethe's Earth Spirit: 'You're like the spirit that you grasp/You're not like me'. [39]

Enough people of talent with a reformist orientation are to be found in the institutions and on their margins, for example in the scientific establishments, who are ready to accept compelling impulses from outside and then propose to the establishment a feasible programme of energy conservation or measures for the humanising of work etc. But this is not an affair for the movement itself. This need only supply the impulse, which need not necessarily be refined and adequate to the problem. The main thing is to produce the pressure: then it is always possible to discuss how progress can be made most effectively and avoiding as far as possible counter-productive diversions.

The movement must not be seduced into becoming 'constructive' and obeying pre-existing patterns, as long as it still has no influence on the basic direction. The practice of Solidarity in Poland has given us a good example of this, in so far as it refused to take responsibility so long as the hostile apparatus still had its hand on the wheel. The movement in the West must stick still more forcefully to a position of fundamental opposition, as here seduction by the pliability of the institutions is far greater than in the East or South.

What the movement offers that is positive and alternative is not something to be attained within the system, but in opposition to it. Even though the eventual outcome will certainly not be a purist one, the movement must strive to completely cast off the ruling structure. In its actual practice, therefore, its own ideal can be present only as the measure by which actions of obstruction are assessed. It must take shape in forms of behaviour, in methods and means, both inwardly and outwardly. Militancy is not the same as violence. Here in the metropolitan countries, at any rate, everything indicates a strategy of non-violence in the sense of not injuring life on the other side. If we force them to use tanks, then we ourselves make the ideological breakthrough impossible.

For those involved, the conversion movement itself becomes an adventure, a field for enjoyment of life and self-realisation and identification. The different society, the new state of the world as a *goal,* is not the ultimate motive of commitment, even though the utopia is very important for the direction as well as for the choice of means. In view of the provocation that the social structure represents for the genotype, the natural human constitution, the goal is as it were newly founded by natural right. The human being has a claim to the satisfaction of the basic social needs that our natural history, our pre-historic biological evolution brought with us into civilisation when this began. In the utopias, whose number is legion, a situation is outlined that precisely promises fulfilment to this.

It is of course impossible, in strictly epistemological terms, to really abstract from the present historical existence of the civilised human being, but this does not prohibit the completely necessary concern to distinguish between things that we can dispense with by our nature and things which we cannot dispense with. Tangible units that are to a large degree autonomous and even autarchic with respect to everyday needs are the ever recurring ideal — an ideal, moreover, that at least in this generalisation is not exclusively designed for industrialised countries. The opposite image is one of large-scale technology and organisation, which are recognised as hostile to individuality, initiative and communication, and where the source of material waste is also to be found. I believe that the resistance of these constants to any critical scathing bears witness to an irrefutable content.

To conclude, and to summarise once again: in East and West and South we are dealing with the different consequences of one and the same challenge, with the formerly unstoppable character of capital accumulation, which however bears with it more than just the dominant social formation of the last two hundred years. In this connection, the economic component that is stressed in the description proves to be only the spearhead of an overall development proceeding from European civilisation, which must unquestionably be corrected if we are to have a future as a species.

The industrialisation-to-death of the world is pursued by an institutional complex of competing camps and states, firms and corporations, which can do nothing else but drive forward the criminal process in *its* direction. There is an international priesthood, including the so-called elites of the Third World, which directly serves the Moloch.

The employers' associations and trade unions in the metropolises also pursue one and the same goal externally, for all their antagonistic cooperation. If a shipyard in my own city of Bremen is threatened with the loss of an order to a Danish shipyard, then all the political and corporate forces unite in demanding state subsidies so that it will be the *German* ship-building industry that increases surplus capacity for sea transport. Let people in other countries go without work! Outside the European borders no consequences of export strategies are foreseen — there things can take their own course. No one *wants* the starving millions who are the natural result of the logic of the world market.

The official structures occupy themselves incessantly with military and industrial competition, with the spread of scientific progress and the stereotyped commercial culture across the whole world, and anyone who is forced to live on this only dies from it a bit more each day.

There are various seemingly irrational responses in vogue: the New Age Movement or the Acquarian Conspiracy. One thing about them is correct: what is required really is a world-embracing counter-movement, and there is *no* Archimedian point within the existing institutions which could be used to bring about even the smallest change of course. Without forces that attack from outside, the atomic holocaust is not to be staved off. It is not a question of the fate of governments on the one hand, movements on the other, not a question of impartial prognoses of their respective chances. What is at stake is the fate of the world, including the fate of these impartial umpires.

I would like to return finally to the point that we must direct ourselves to the real and in no way ethereal function that the prophetic invocation of God always had in apocalyptic situations: as the authoritative and visionary appeal to a radical change of consciousness, to a break with the death-dealing habits that compel us to play along with everything so that tomorrow there will still be power for the electric shaver. The question is to give this appeal a content, character and style that is in keeping with the times. If we have come to view a certain kind of enlightenment and science as contemptible, I still believe that we should act in a manner that in no way rejects the legacy of reason.

Talk at the World Future Studies Federation in Stockholm, June 1982

Notes

(All notes are by the translator.)

1   The title given to *Die Alternative* in English suggests that its scope is confined simply to the countries of the Soviet bloc; but see below, p. 18.

2   Bahro uses the term *'Wertkonservativen'* as opposed to the *'Strukturkonservativen'* whose allegiance is to present social structures rather than to the values these are deemed to embody. The dichotomy is taken from Erhard Eppler — see note 26.

3   *Der Spiegel,* 22 October 1979.

4   This Socialist Conference was held in Kassel in May 1980, at Bahro's initiative. Follow-up conferences have been held since.

5   In the 1979 elections to the Bremen *Landtag,* the Green list won more than 5 per cent of the votes and thus obtained representation.

6   Carl Amery is a leading figure in the Green movement, and author of *Natur als Politik.*

7   The seminary at Tübingen was where Hegel first studied.

8   *The Alternative in Eastern Europe* (New Left Books: 1978), p.411.

9   Karl Marx, *Capital* Vol. 3 (Pelican Marx Library: 1981), pp.958-9.

10   See above, pp.22-3.

11   Like the formation of the Green party, the Multicoloured *(Bunte)* and Alternative lists came together in preparation for the October 1980 Federal elections.

12   *The Alternative in Eastern Europe,* p. 305.

13   Antonin Novotny was the Stalinist first secretary of the Czechoslovak Communist Party, forced to resign by the 'Prague spring'.

14   After the Spartacus League, the predecessor of the German Communist Party founded by Rosa Luxemburg and Karl Liebknecht, which launched a brave but untimely insurrection in January 1919.

15   The largest of the new generation of Marxist-Leninist groups, the KPD, did dissolve itself, its leadership recommending members to join the Green party.

16 This refers to an article by Ernest Mandel and Jakob Moneta, 'Vom Kampf der Klassen zum Kampf der Blöcke' in *Kritik* 25 (West Berlin: 1980).

17 Wolfgang Harich, an East German philosopher exiled to Austria, has also identified himself with the Green movement. On Herbert Gruhl, see above, p.14.

18 Bernd Rabehl's critique of Bahro was published in *Kritik* 23 (West Berlin: 1980).

19 See J.W. Goethe, *Faust* Part Two (Penguin: 1975), pp. 76-9 and 15.

20 Bahro frequently uses the word 'conversion' *(Umkehr)*, with deliberate allusion to its religious overtone. See p.58, and pp.143 ff.

21 Giuseppe de Lampedusa, in his novel *The Leopard*.

22 This Russian industrialist, who died in 1905, left 60,000 roubles to the Bolshevik party.

23 See above, p. 74.

24 'Einige zaghafte Einwände gegen den linken Pessimismus', *Freibeuter* 1 (West Berlin: 1979).

25 Schiller's poem narrates a 'winter journey' through Germany under the post-Napoleonic reaction.

26 Erhard Eppler is a member of the SPD executive, and a supporter of the Green cause and the peace movement within the SPD.

27 See above, pp. 85-6.

28 Bahro acknowledges a debt to Gorz's writings, which he read only after arriving in the West. The title 'Goodbye to Capitalism...' (p. 62) is a reference to Gorz's latest work.

29 'Pflicht für jeden', in 'Tabulae Votivae von Schiller und Goethe'; Schiller, *Sämtliche Werke* Vol. 1 (Munich: 1965), p. 305.

30 Edward Thompson, 'Notes on Exterminism, the Last Stage of Civilisation', *New Left Review* 121 (London: 1980).

31 *The Revolutions of 1848* (Pelican Marx Library: 1973), p. 71.

32 'Critique of Hegel's Philosophy of Right. Introduction'; *Early Writings* (Pelican Marx Library: 1975), p. 257.

33 K. Marx and F. Engels, *Collected Works* Vol. 5 (Lawrence & Wishart: 1976), p. 49.

34 F. Schiller, 'Die Sendung des Moses', *Sämtliche Werke* Vol. 4 (Munich: 1962), p. 787.

35 Bahro is himself the author of an essay on Beethoven, *Die nicht mit den Wölfen heulen* (Cologne: 1979).

36 *Trades' Unions and Strikes: Their Philosophy and Intention* (London: 1860), quoted by Marx in *Capital* Vol. 1 (Pelican Marx Library: 1976), p. 926.

37 *Faust* Part Two (loc. cit.), p. 265.
38 Bertold Brecht, *Poems* [ed. Willett/Mannheim/Fried] (Methuen 1976), p. 291.
39 J.W. Goethe, Faust Part One (Bantam: 1967), pp. 33-5 (lines 512 -3).